Parris Island Daze

My Drill Instructor Was Tougher Than Yours

Robert E. Shirley

Copyright © 2006 by Robert E. Shirley

All rights reserved. No part of this book shall be reproduced or transmitted in any form or by any means, electronic, mechanical, magnetic, photographic including photocopying, recording or by any information storage and retrieval system, without prior written permission of the publisher. No patent liability is assumed with respect to the use of the information contained herein. Although every precaution has been taken in the preparation of this book, the publisher and author assume no responsibility for errors or omissions. Neither is any liability assumed for damages resulting from the use of the information contained herein.

ISBN 0-7414-3504-7

Published by:

1094 New DeHaven Street, Suite 100
West Conshohocken, PA 19428-2713
Info@buybooksontheweb.com
www.buybooksontheweb.com
Toll-free (877) BUY BOOK
Local Phone (610) 941-9999
Fax (610) 941-9959

Printed in the United States of America
Printed on Recycled Paper
Published September 2006

For my Ragtime Gal

for my dear friend and Army veteran Dave Haberle,
the toughest soldier I've ever known

to the memory of my drill instructor, Richard A. Lance;
he made a difference

and for Marines everywhere – Semper Fi!

Contents

CHAPTER 1 – LET THE GAMES BEGIN

Lightning Strike in Yemassee	1
For What We Are About to Receive	6
Mattress Walk	10

CHAPTER 2 – MAKING NEW FRIENDS

And Grab Your Socks	15
A Riveting Experience	19
The General's Orders	22
Meeting Our DIs	24

CHAPTER 3 – SETTLING IN

Sit, You Heathens	28
Putting On the Right Face	31
Let Them Wear Skivvies	33
Home, Sweet Home	36
Shopping Spree	40
Letters to Mommy	44

CHAPTER 4 – TESTING, 1, 2

Turn and Cough	49
Make a Muscle	51
Let's Take a Dip	53
You're In the Infantry, Turd	57

CHAPTER 5 – WE NEED MORE STUFF

Good Mornin' World	61
Ricochet to Forest Lawn	66
Holiday on Asphalt	69
He's Not Heavy	72

CHAPTER 6 – DOWN TO BUSINESS

Command Performance	74
I Have Not Yet Begun To Exercise	78
Darrell Dottle	80

CHAPTER 7 – CLEAN UP YOUR ROOM

Field Day	83
Mowing the Grass	85
Duz does Everything	88
A Dirty, Disgusting Habit	90
A Little Serutan, Please	92

CHAPTER 8 – A LITTLE EDUCATION IS A GOOD THING

The World, According to Hoot	93
Getting Religion	97
Marching With the Junior Birdmen	100

CHAPTER 9 – SNAKE STRIKES AGAIN, AND AGAIN

Things That Go Bump	104
Life Is Just a Box of Cherries	106

CHAPTER 10 – REFLECTIONS 110
   Happy Hour 110
   Getting To Know You 112
   My Fellow Turds 113

CHAPTER 11 – WHO GOES THERE?
   No Fire or Disorder That I Can See 120
   Sleep Walk 121
   Nod if You Agree 125
   People in India are Starving 128
   The Eyes of Platoon 2037 Are Upon You ... 135

CHAPTER 12 – THESE ARE THE TIMES THAT TRY MENS SOLES
   Just Go Ahead and Have a Big Tea Party ... 138
   Smile and the Whole World Doesn't Smile With You 141
   Who's From Philly? 145
   It's Party Time! 147
   Help, Chesty! 150

CHAPTER 13 – AND ON WITH THE SHOW
   Second Wind 156
   Letters, He Gets Letters 160
   Get Lost, Buster! 162

CHAPTER 14 – DOOM AND GLOOM
   Showdown at the Triangle PX 165
   Requiem for a Downed Flyer 167
   Reservation for Cpl. Winston 170
   Telephone Pole, Anyone? 175

CHAPTER 15 – RIFLE RANGE

Cheek to Cheek	181
The Sport of Turds	185
Winning Our Sandspurs	188
Dance, Buckaroo	190
Buffalo in the Butts	192
Hi Honey, Here I am!	197
Silk Skivvies	198

CHAPTER 16 – FINAL PHASE

A Night at the Beach	204
A Pillaging We Will Go	208
The Midnight Gardener	213
Cpl. Winston's Deposit	216
How Ya Gonna Keep 'Em Down On the Farm?	217
For He's A Jolly Good Fellow	220
I'm Pretty Sure I'm Confident	221
My Report Card	226

CHAPTER 17 – VENI, VIDI, VICI

My Pride Runneth Over	229
Give Me Liberty	234
The Beat Goes On	235

Epilogue	238
Glossary	241
Parris Island Reading List	246
Send Me Your Funny Boot Camp Story	247

Acknowledgments

I'm grateful to each and every one of the many people who helped me along the way to publish this book. Any errors are mine and mine alone.

First, thanks to my dear wife Karen, who always believed in the book.

I'd also especially like to thank Bill Hughes of the Marine Corps Association, Chuck Taliano, former DI and whose picture appears on the cover of this book, Major Margaret Miller Weitzel, USMC, Ann Kempner Fisher, Dr. Steve Wise of the Parris Island Museum, Dr. Eugene Alvarez, Cmdr. Robert F. Nevin, USN (ret.), and Mike Waldron.

I'd like to thank the Marine Corps Association for the cover photo and the United States Marine Corps for the many photos used in the book. Thanks to the members of the Nassau (Florida) and Kings Bay (Georgia) Detachments of the Marine Corps League for giving me the inspiration to write this book.

Prologue

Before you woke up this morning, 4,000 young men and women already had breakfast, given their drill instructor twenty pushups, and probably marched a couple of miles. It's enough to make these early birds a little grumpy.

On the other hand, they are recruits at the Marine Corps Recruit Depot at Parris Island, and have no right to be happy. Not in boot camp. They are there to shed the skin of civilian life, grow up, and become Marines. But be forewarned, unauthorized and unexpected as it may be, some of these recruits *may be undercover smilers*.

When Marines get together to swap sea stories, the subject eventually turns to the Parris Island experience. There's a lot of pleasant bantering as to who had the toughest drill instructor, the more frugal living conditions, and how much harder it was in the "Old Corps." Recently I swapped sea stories with a dozen 18- and 19-year-old graduates of 2006. One had the gall to tell me *his* DI was tougher than mine. Whether it happened years ago or yesterday, it's a shared experience that changed our lives forever.

Now, before memories fade, I want to describe a lighter side of Parris Island. Other than the generally accepted version where sadistic drill instructors abuse, brainwash, and humiliate recruits for their own pleasure. This book is about one recruit's humorous observations and reactions to the daily pressures, both mental and physical, of boot camp.

It's a one-sided sea story that I especially want to share with all my Marine buddies who went through Parris Island and San Diego, as well as the millions of soldiers, sailors, and airmen who went through their own boot camps. Reminisce with me, and smile or chuckle about those almost-forgotten, impossible situations and zany DI insults. True, the situations and insults weren't as funny then, but they're definitely funny now.

Although several fine books have been written on the factual side, there hasn't been a humorous window to Parris Island since *Gomer Pyle*. My second objective in writing this book is that I hope that recruits' family members will also find something to snicker about when they learn what their husbands, sons, daughters, brothers and sisters went, or are going, through. And to find something to be proud about.

My PI experience taught me that all of us have a degree of courage and of toughness that can be tempered. It taught me guts, endurance, and patience. It taught me to reach deep within myself and find the confidence and stick-to-it-iveness to grit out difficult assignments. I learned and adopted a motto which I use to this day: "we will prevail." We can get anything done if we work together or, if need be, by ourselves.

My Parris Island experience changed me from a shy, retiring runt into a sometimes brash, participating, semi-runt. From a lemming into a sometimes leader. I learned that, in spite of being insulted, exhausted, and pressured, I could still function. I wasn't a glutton for punishment, but I was open to learn how to endure a fair measure of stress and still get the job done. Life is full of challenges. Shit happens.

Some people say "Gyyreeenee" is the sound you hear when the compost hits the fan. A generous portion of that compost is scattered across Parris Island.

Former Georgia Governor Zell Miller wrote a book called *Corps Values: Everything You Need to Know I Learned in the Marines*. I agree that all I needed to learn, about *how to learn*, I learned at Parris Island. More about what I learned and how Parris Island has changed later, but right now it's time to report in.

CHAPTER 1 – LET THE GAMES BEGIN

Lightning Strike in Yemassee

October 2, 1958

I knew that I'd made a colossal mistake within the first five seconds after our train arrived at the Yemassee, South Carolina depot. It was a mistake with the crack and sizzle of a thunderbolt that streaks across the sky and singes the seat of your trousers.

As the Atlantic Coast Line train screeched to a halt, the bright overhead lights flashed on. I blinked and rubbed my eyes as two Marine Military Policemen (MPs) dressed in starched khaki uniforms and red armbands leaped aboard my rail car.

"All Marine Corps recruits will stand up and get off the train," they bellowed, "all Marine recruits for Parris Island! Get up and get off the train! Now!"

The MPs rushed down the aisle beating the tops of the cloth seats with their billy clubs, causing clouds of dust to rise in the eerie light.

My body developed instant paralysis and my heart leapt in my chest. The MPs stormed down the aisle, making direct eye contact with each passenger. One MP looked left; the other looked to the right.

"Are you a Marine recruit," one MP demanded, shaking a dozing young man. The recruit rubbed his eyes and mumbled a sleepy "yes." He was instantly jerked to his feet and propelled down the aisle. One after another, the half-awake recruits were yanked to their feet and shoved toward the exit steps, their duffel bags and hats sailing after them.

The elderly Miami-bound couples hugged each other and looked on with gaping mouths as the MPs continued clubbing the seat tops, driving the recruits toward my end of the car. The recruits bumped into seats and into each other, struggling to reach the exit, accompanied by groans, occasional whimpers, and barely audible curses.

As the MPs neared my seat, something must have vacuumed all the air out of the railcar, because I had to fight to suck in each breath. I felt dizzy and light-headed as I dragged myself to my feet. My crewneck sweater collar squeezed my neck like a noose and I felt my pulse pounding against the fabric.

"On your feet! Get up and get off! Come on, hurry up, hurry up! Better get moving, Sonny, before you get help! You better not be the last one off! Move! Move!"

To encourage the recruits to take their "suggestion" seriously, the MPs physically assisted the recruits and their luggage off the train. All sixty of us exited the train and landed on the platform with our duffel bags in less than thirty seconds. This little impromptu stampede spoke volumes for their efficiency. That some of the luggage didn't belong to us didn't seem to matter.

I wondered if an eighteen-year-old could develop heart trouble or instant paralysis without a stroke. How about instant emphysema without ever smoking?

As the train spun its wheels in its haste to pull away from the platform, the MPs stampeded our ragged mob, herding us across the platform and onto a small parking lot next to a one-story cottage. The exodus resembled waves of small fish that instantly change direction when a predator threatens.

One minute after one in the morning and these guys are trying to set records. Unlike the Marines in the recruiting posters, none of them were dressed in blue uniforms, or carried swords or anything. No "glad to see ya," no "Hi buddy," no handshaking, nothing. No, the message was clear: "the Marine Corps builds men, and we're starting this morning."

A lean, thin-lipped Marine stood waiting, tapping his pencil on a clipboard. "You have arrived at Yemassee, South Carolina," he snarled. "Major General Rufus Hauling, Commanding General of the Marine Corps Recruit Depot at Parris Island, welcomes you. You will be transported presently by bus to the Island."

Our greeter stalked around our midst, counting and scowling. As he passed, I noticed his two stripes were new, but didn't cover a larger space on his sleeve that once had been covered by *three* stripes. Not a good sign. Evidently he, too, had been recently scorched by a thunderbolt.

Greeter stopped in front of a recruit and grabbed one of his hands. "Take your hands out of your pockets, Skippy! You playing pocket pool?"

Greeter circled the herd, shoving, screaming, and correcting the posture of the recruits. Resuming his place at the head of the group, he mechanically continued his welcoming lecture.

"You will stand up straight! No talking! No chewing gum! No smoking. No moving around. Keep your eyes to the front!"

He abruptly turned and strutted into the little cottage, no doubt to inform the general we had arrived. The MPs guarded both sides of the mob, tapping their billy clubs in their palms, making sure none escaped.

We stood at mob attention, cursing ourselves for not having joined the Coast Guard. Or maybe the Army; at least the Army's recruiting poster said *they* wanted us. There we stood, one o'clock in the morning, tired, without a neighborly face in sight, and in the hands of testy overachievers.

I tried to will my thudding heart and breathing back to normal. Okay, calm down, calm down. Maybe these guys were pissed about having to leave a nice warm bed, get all dressed up, and collect a bunch of civilians. They hadn't actually beaten us with the billy clubs. No one had been bodily thrown from the train, although I did play pinball with the exit stairs and missed a couple of steps as they "encouraged" me to get off.

Maybe they were just eager to get started. Maybe they were looking forward to returning to their soft warm bed partners. Maybe they just didn't like civilians. I prayed they weren't going to be our drill instructors and that the next bunch of Marines would be human.

A mist began to fall, but the herd members were still too much in shock or too lost in remorse to notice, or care. Careful not to get their creased uniforms wet, the MPs stepped back under the depot overhang.

After a few halfhearted spurts, the rain came down with conviction and continued for a half hour or so. It trickled off my hair and down my neck, sending a stream of chilled water coursing down my back. My body shuddered and my back tensed with the shock. Or was it fear?

When the rain slacked off to a drizzle, our greeter waltzed out, looking vaguely surprised.

"Why didn't someone come in and tell me it was raining out here," he asked, glancing at his clipboard. "You people didn't have to stand out here in the rain!" He didn't look very broken up about it.

First, he says no moving about, then no talking. Now he says why didn't someone move around, talk, and generally throw a fraternity party in the darned little building? These people were impossible to please.

A beat up Greyhound bus lurched out of the dark swamps and Greeter stuffed all sixty of us in it. This surprised me, as I thought buses carried only forty or so.

After seeing the recruits safely on the bus, the MPs retired to their pickup trucks and spun gravel in their haste to get back to their bed partners. Almost like they didn't want to be witnesses for what might happen next.

The bus took off in a cloud of diesel smoke and bounced along in the darkness. I tried to see out between elbows and duffel bags, but could only glimpse foggy swampage and a bridge over a creek. Greeter barked that there were sharks and gators in the water and several recruits had tried to swim it, but no one had made it yet.

The bus was as silent as a cattle rustler's hanging on a foggy morning. No one dared speak with the short-tempered Greeter perched on the front step, glaring out the windshield. We resigned ourselves to the trip, breathing in fumes of damp clothing, tobacco, and disinfectant.

I wondered if we were passing the swamp where six recruits had drowned two years ago during a night punishment march. My father, who worked in a Pennsylvania steel mill, had heard from his buddy that a Drill Instructor (DI) had smashed out all of his son's teeth with a rifle butt. Probably for falling asleep at 1 a.m.

The bus droned on and on, deeper and deeper into the gloom of moss covered live oaks and swampy marshes, deeper into the Transylvania of the South.

It worried me now that I didn't memorize my eleven "general orders." The recruiting sergeant had told us we had better learn them on the train before we showed up. I *did know* one of them, though; one of the four shortest ones. I'd be all right if they started with number eight: "To give the alarm in case of fire or disorder."

Judas Priest. What had I gotten myself into?

The seat of my pants was still trailing a thin wisp of smoke from the thunderbolt as I was spirited into the United States Marine Corps Recruit Depot, Parris Island.

For What We Are About to Receive

The Greyhound hissed loudly and ground to a halt in front of a two-story red brick building. Looking back at us over his shoulder, Greeter jumped off into a puddle, simultaneously turning his ankle. He spoke a few words in a "forceful" manner, damning the Marine Corps, the hour, the bus, the bus driver, us, and generally gave us to understand that we had better get the hell off the goddammed bus, up the stairs and into the doors of the illegitimate building. Needing no further words of encouragement, we stumbled off the bus and surged towards the steps.

I was tempted to ask the bus driver to keep the motor running, but he was intensely contemplating his fingernails and did not look up.

Before we could reach the building, the doors banged open. Two of Greeter's ill tempered, foul-mouthed associates in Smokey Bear hats charged down the stairs. Grabbing our arms, shouting in our faces, and jerking and shoving us into the building, they had to be relatives of the welcoming committee at the train station.

"Get up there, you worthless piece of civilian shit! Move it! Move it! Are you staring at me? Keep your eyes straight ahead! Quit that sniveling! Are you a little *girl*? You better get your goddammed ass in that door! Hurry up! You want me to help you, maggot? You better not be the *last one* through that hatch!"

"Get in the classroom! Move! Move! Move! Find a seat and stand by it! At *attention*! Get in there!"

Choking, gasping, and yelping sounds surrounded me as we were jostled, pushed, and yanked up the stairs into the hallway, and propelled into a classroom. The two goons rushed around the room, yanking recruits to empty seats, shouting into their faces, punching guts to improve posture, and screaming invective to some whose hair was too long, clothes too flashy, or facial expressions too calm.

Some "lucky" local recruits arriving in the daytime.
Photo courtesy of United States Marine Corps.

Finally, after we were all "welcomed," Greeter nodded to the goon squad and they stalked, glaring and muttering, out of the room.

The whole abortive exercise couldn't have taken more than thirty seconds and *still* they were unhappy. Probably wasn't their personal best time.

Greeter strutted leisurely to the front of the classroom and lounged at an old wooden "teacher's" desk. The speed trial rules apparently didn't apply to him.

"Sit! At attention! Straighten your back! No talking!

No moving! Keep your eyes to the front!"

We sat, at what we hoped was attention, in small wooden classroom chairs with arms. A sign on the wall said "Quiet" but wasn't needed. The only sounds were panting and my pulse pounding again in my ears; the smell of floor wax, chalk and damp clothing invading my nostrils.

"I will now call out the names of those recruits designated in charge of your recruiting station. When I call your name, you will sound off 'Here, Sir!' loud and clear, and get your ass up here with your orders. You will sound off only if *all* of your people are here. You were ordered to show up with all of your people, or not at all. Therefore, the only acceptable answer is 'Here, Sir.'"

"Pendergast," Greeter shouted.

"Me," our bespectacled representative for Pittsburgh inquired, "Pendergast?"

"No, *me Pendergast*," Greeter rasped, "how many Pendergasts you think are here? The first word out of your mouth is 'Sir', Dumbass! If your name is Pendergast and if you are from Pittsburgh, you will answer 'here, sir'! Sound off!"

"Here, sir," Pendergast admitted.

"*Here, sir*," Greeter mimicked sweetly, "what the hell's the matter with you, Four Eyes; your shorts too tight? This is *not* the Girl Scouts and I'm *not* your Den Mother! Speak up!"

"Here, sir," Four Eyes screamed.

"Arright, Four Eyes," Greeter screamed back, leaning over his desk, "you waiting for a *personal invitation*? Get your ass up here!"

Greeter quickly checked in the various recruiting stations without major incident until he called for the Cleveland representative.

"Sonsini, Cleveland," Greeter barked.

Cleveland, a large sullen fellow, slouched in his chair and muttered a Marlon Brando style "Yeah."

A khaki blur whipped passed me as Greeter erupted out of his chair, shot to the back of the classroom, and jerked Cleveland out of his chair. Cleveland's chair overturned and clanged against the floor, inspiring the rest of us to sit up even straighter. Greeter pinned the chair's former occupant against the back wall, his hand on Cleveland's throat.

"Yeah? *Yeah*," Greeter shrieked, his face an inch from Cleveland's, "who in the hell do you think you're talking to? Your father? Your teacher? A police officer? You're talking to a *Marine*, you smartass civilian piece of *shit*!"

I kept my eyes straight ahead, my back straight, and prayed my panting would not attract Greeter's attention. I tried to look humble and reverent, nothing like Brando.

"You're not going to make it, Hood!" Greeter punched him in the stomach. "You better *sound off*!" He gave the hood another punch in the gut. "And sound off *now*!" And another punch. "Because there won't be any more chances!" One more punch. "I'll kick your ass till your teeth rattle! Sound *off*!"

Cleveland struggled to speak, his Adam's apple pinched in Greeter's grasp. "Goddammit, you better say *something*, and I hope to Christ it's '*yeah!*'"

"Here, Sir," Cleveland croaked.

"I can't hear you, *pussy*," Greeter sneered, his spit flecking Cleveland's face. "You talk like a little girl. *Sound off*!"

"*Pussy*"? *Pussy*? We didn't say "pussy" where I came from. Sometimes the really tough kids said that, but it was taboo to utter nasty words like "pussy."

"Here, Sir," Cleveland rasped with conviction.

Greeter released Cleveland's throat and strode back to his desk. "Get your ass up here, turd."

The turd broke the record for the ten-yard dash up to Greeter's desk, stood as straight as a ramrod, and wisely restrained himself from further Brando imitations.

Well, I prayed, maybe the next bunch of Marines would be human.

Mattress Walk

After recording all the groups, Greeter introduced us to our next tormentor, a green fireplug with a Smokey Bear hat, but no neck. He too, didn't beat around the bush.

"Okay, turds, my name's Sgt. O' Brien and I'm the *toughest* sonofabitch on this island." He surveyed the lot of us, checking reactions. "Which one of you bad asses doesn't think so?"

Everybody must have thought so, or maybe felt sorry for him being illegitimate, because nobody said shit. He brightened a little, probably relieved that there were no Golden Glove boxers in the lot. He swaggered around the classroom, stopping in front of our biggest miserable turd.

Looking up about a foot, he shouted into the big turd's Adam's apple, "How about you, Tiny? Do you want to try me? Hunh? *Hunh*?"

Tiny swallowed and sat even straighter, but said nothing. Or maybe could not.

"You girls are nothing but a bunch of worthless civilian shit," Sgt. O'Brien continued. "How in the *hell* you managed to bullshit our recruiters is beyond me. They must have stumbled upon the bowels of America that spawned you turds. Goddamn waste of the taxpayers' money to feed and house you civilian rejects."

"Okay," O'Brien said, looking at his watch, "in a minute we're all going to rush topside, I mean upstairs. I almost forgot myself there. I'm used to being around Marines. I'm going to tuck all your little asses in, just like your mommies did back home. When I say the word, you people will get upstairs! Move out! Up the stairs on your left! Get moving! You need some help, Sweetie?"

We scurried topside into a large room full of double deck bunk beds. Each bed consisted of a steel rectangle with a single lace of tightly stretched wire springs. A 2-inch thick mattress was rolled like a sausage at one end, covered by a matching 2-inch thick pillow. Both looked like they had been stamped out by the same steamroller.

We filed by a door where sheets and pillowcases sailed out on 3-second intervals. I never did see if somebody threw them, or if they owned an automatic sheet thrower. Anyway, we all got our bedding and lined up along the walls.

"When I say the word," O'Brien bellowed, "each crud will find herself a rack and put her gear on it. There may not be enough racks so some of you may have to bunk on the deck. We don't allow you girls to sleep together, so tell each of your little friends 'nightie-night' now. Arright, go get a rack!"

The mad scramble that followed saw several racks wavering in tugs of war, half a dozen cruds trampled, and at the end, two or three cruds searching frantically like trapped rats for the remaining racks.

Sgt. O'Brien was of no help, stalking in the midst of the confusion, shoving turds and screaming for us to hurry up, hurry up. Surprising, there were more than enough racks for everyone and no one had to sleep on the floor.

O'Brien slowly shook his head, disgusted by our performance in his private mice maze, and called us over to watch him make up a rack. In less than two minutes, he had the rack made up. After tucking in the corners of the sheet hospital style and tightening the blanket into a tight rectangle with a white bib on it, he threw a penny in the middle of the blanket. It bounced.

"That's how *every* rack will be made," he stated confidently, "most of you girls have never made a bed in your life, but Mommy isn't here to do it for you tonight." He glanced at his watch.

"You people have five minutes to make up these racks. If they are made up when I come back, you can all go nightie-nite." He glanced at his watch again.

"You now have four minutes and forty-five seconds. Get hot!"

I unrolled the so-called mattress and worked like a madman to get the sheet corners square. I got two corners on one end fairly respectable and decided that would be the head. I hid the rejects under the blanket and quickly tidied up the masterpiece.

Except for looking like a bowed hot dog roll, the rack vaguely resembled the good sergeant's example and the penny even managed a feeble bounce. I was in the process of trying to overpower the hot dog roll when Sgt. O'Brien marched into the room.

"You girls can't even learn to make up your racks let alone learn how to march or fire a weapon," the toughest sonofabitch on the island declared.

"My three-year-old kid can make a rack better than the best one here," O'Brien grumbled.

It wasn't hard thinking of Sgt. O'Brien blowing a whistle and having his kids line up in front of their beds. Fun for the whole family.

"At home you probably just crawled into a burlap sack. Well, tear 'em up and make 'em again. This time you got four minutes!"

I really felt bad about ruining my neat job and hesitated to see if I could salvage part of it, but when I saw Sgt. O'Brien ripping up a few of the slow starter's racks, I tore into the job.

This time the hotdog was worse and I know that I would have suffered something unpleasant if Sgt. O'Brien hadn't gotten disgusted before he reached my rack. A mattress and its sheets went sailing through the air, then another, and another.

"Arright, girls, arright," he nodded sagely, "I know what the trouble is. You people have too much energy to do a simple delicate thing like making a rack. The anticipation of training at the world's finest military training camp has all of your little hearts beating double time. A little exercise will help put you at ease, steady your hand, and maybe take off an ounce or two of your goddamn civilian baby fat."

"We're going to play a little game. You girls like games? Oh, I love games," he enthused, "let's play – Mattress Walk! Now pay attention so you girls get it the first time. Pick up your mattress! Now place it on your head. That's it, Sweetie; you are one of my quick learners! Does everyone understand? Goodie! Now line up along the wall. That's right, Numb One, just run into the bulkhead! Are you fuckin' *blind*?"

"Fuckin'?" Did I hear him right? Did he say "fuckin'?" What kind of vocabulary did these people have? First "pussy," now "fuckin'." Miss Biddy, my high school English teacher, had lectured me one day for half an hour after overhearing me say "shit." Seems I didn't have sufficient command of the Queen's English, causing me to resort to such filth. She would have a field day with this study. And what the heck was a "bulkhead?"

"Okay, when I say the word, you will run around the bulkhead until I think you are ready to get your shit together. Then we'll stop and try pitching pennies again. Won't that be swell? Okay, get moving! Move! Move! Close it up! Move! Move! *Move!*"

He shoved a couple of slow starters.

Although I ran like a panther, my shins kept getting barked by the guy in front of me, and the guy in back kept pushing his mattress into my head, keeping me off balance. After ten painful laps around the room, the good sergeant decided that some of us might like to try for an even dozen, so told us to halt.

A few turds had defective hearing, or else didn't understand even the most elementary German, and crashed into those who had stopped.

We were given another chance at appeasing Sgt. O'Brien and again tried to make the infernal racks to his 3-year-old's standard. We did a little better, but still not good enough to excuse us from another mattress walk. As we put in ten more laps, my bruised shins and I wondered why it wasn't called the mattress *run*.

Finally, on the third time, we managed to please the rotten deformed sadist and we were allowed to actually lie down on the rack. Unbelievable as it were, Sgt. O'Brien went away, probably to inspect his poor little kid's rack. The lights went out and we all fell gratefully into unconsciousness.

It was 4:20 a.m., only three hours and twenty minutes since we had left the safety of the train.

Years later I found out that the Corps deliberately scheduled the arrival of most new recruits in the middle of the night. Disoriented turds are easier to manage. Only recruits from the local recruiting areas arrive by bus in the daytime.

CHAPTER 2 – MAKING NEW FRIENDS

And Grab Your Socks

"Drop your cocks and grab your socks! Reveille! Reveille!"

Sgt. O'Brien stood in the doorway, running a club around the inside of a large galvanized garbage can, while some idiot stood beside him, blaring a horn.

"Outa the racks! Let's go, *on your feet!*"

We bounded out of our racks and stood around half awake, ready to play mattress walk again. It was 5:00 a.m. Forty minutes after lights out.

Eyeing a couple of late risers, O'Brien picked up the garbage can and threw it twenty feet into the room before it bounced and careened off two or three racks.

"Did we enjoy our little naps," he asked sweetly, glancing at his watch. "It's oh-five-hundred; that's when the Marine Corps wakes up. We have a big day ahead of us, so you have thirty minutes to shit, shower and shave!"

"Thirty minutes from now, I'm going to walk through that door. And when I do, the first turd to see me will drop what he's doing and sound off 'standby.' When the rest of you girls hear him say 'standby,' you will yell 'attention.' Do you have that? When – no, rather than waste my time repeating myself and hoping you assholes remember it for thirty minutes, we'll try it now."

Whereas he walked out of the room, turned and started back for the doorway.

"Standby," a couple of the turds shouted.

"Attention," the rest of us thundered.

Sgt. O'Brien, however, stopped a foot or two before he entered the room. Now he sauntered in, shaking his head.

"You dumb shits! What've you got, shit for brains? I said when I came *through* the door. Nobody came through the door. And when I *did* come through the door, nobody said shit!"

He glared at the roomful of excrement packed craniums and snorted. He glanced at his watch.

"When I come through that door, in twenty-nine minutes, I better hear it loud and clear, and next time I want it *right*! You'll stay here all day if it ain't, and we can get in a lot of 'standby, attentions' before taps."

He consulted his watch again. "You girls better shape up if you wanta go to chow. You only got twenty-eight minutes now."

With that parting shot, he left us to compete over the six sinks in the bathroom, which had to be shared by eight to ten guys apiece. At 5 feet, 8 inches, I was one of the little shavers and was quickly pushed to the rear of the lines.

"Hey, buddy," I asked the first guy in line at the nearest sink, "is it okay if I stand beside you? I have an electric shaver and I won't get in your way or use any of your water."

"Get the hell in the back of the line," the turd in position number two snarled, "you got nothing to shave anyway."

It was true, at eighteen, I shaved only once a week, mostly for show, but I was told to shave, and nothing was going to keep me from shaving.

I tried all the other first placers with approximately the same results. The management was making the guests downright unfriendly. Everybody seemed to be taking about five minutes to shave, which left me ten minutes in the red on even the shortest line.

Going to get a free meal. Photo of courtesy of United States Marine Corps.

I was in deep shit. Maybe they'd dry shave me like I heard they did sometimes, tearing chunks of my peaches 'n' cream skin off like the peel off an orange. I ran into the rack room and looked for a plug. I found an outlet about six inches off the floor and had to kneel to make the cord reach. Without a mirror, it was mostly touch and mow. The strategy saved the day and I was ready to lend my lungs for the "standby, attention" almost a minute ahead of time.

Exactly on time, the Smiling Irishman waltzed into the room. We were on our toes and thundered our hallelujahs in the prescribed manner. He put his hairy paws on his hips and surveyed us with a scornful gaze.

"I'm gonna take you people to chow now. From the looks of some of you that's the only reason you joined up. This is your one and only *free* meal. You didn't do one single goddammed thing to earn it!"

I thought I had earned at least one meal from my short career as a mattress walker and punching bag, but I guess not.

"Some of you turds might think you're gonna sponge off my Corps for the next three or four years, but this is the last handout. It's going to be a big shock to most of you, but we don't walk the streets in our pretty blue uniforms all the time. You turds think you're gonna go home in fancy blue uniforms and make the twits in your home town go all weak in the knees. But you will probably never see a blue uniform as half of you will wash out in a day or two and be sent home to Mommy."

"Okay, get downstairs and clutter up my street in two rows. I'll be right behind you to help those of you that don't understand what I'm talking about. Which is most of you. Get out! Move! Move! Move!"

We ran down the stairs and lined up on the street with the technical assistance, some verbal but mostly physical, of

Sgt. O'Brien. I was shoved along almost the entire length of the line, with the rest of the other pint-sized jarheads. As it was, being at the front of the line only shortened the wait for the famed creamed chipped beef on toast, also known as "SOS," or "shit on a shingle."

As the only group in civilian clothes, we were somewhat intimidated by the sea of green clad groups tramping around us. We hurried along the chow line and found seats where we ravished our SOS. I didn't think I'd be asking for the recipe.

"Well you certainly took your sweetass old time." Sgt. O'Brien growled as we returned to the street. "I didn't say sit around and marvel at the Marines and get autographs. Now you only have five minutes to get back and turn in your skuzzy sheets before your drill instructors come to pick up your sorry asses."

We turned in our skuzzy sheets and rolled our mattresses, but then were allowed to go out on a screened-in porch to smoke.

Some of the recruits that had been there a couple of days said there was word that a couple of recruits had been shot. It seemed that two recruits went berserk and tried to escape. Two drill instructors chased them down with rifles, herding them like sheep. Then, when the recruits broke into a full run, one drill instructor took two shots and brought them both down. Their bodies were dragged to the swamp and thrown in for the alligators.

I was about to ask who saw them do that when the call came for all recruits to get below into the classroom with duffel bags.

A Riveting Experience

After spending a few minutes in our sitting attention position, a giant skinhead wearing a Smokey Bear hat clomped into the classroom, followed by a smaller skinhead giant, also wearing a Smoky Bear hat.

"On your feet," the smaller giant bellowed, "don't you people know to sound attention when a drill instructor enters the room? Sound off!"

"Standby," we chorused, "Attention!"

"Too fuckin' late *now*," the larger giant lectured, "besides, I can't fuckin' *hear* you!"

"What are you," the smaller of the giants taunted, "a bunch of panty waists? Can'tcha talk? You sound like a bunch of Campfire Girls! Standby, attention," he mimicked the nearest recruit.

He went on to yell at the recruit for being cross-eyed or something, but I soon forgot about him, because the big giant was clomping toward my chair. I had fought dearly for a seat at the back of the room where I felt a slight degree of safety. It was now being invaded by the enemy. His bug-eyed, double-chinned face reminded me of a leering frog.

"What the hell are you looking at?" His face jumped in front of mine. "Are you looking at me, turd?"

I could smell his after-shave and sweat and leather. My vocal cords constricted and my heart did a chorus of the mambo.

"No, sir," I managed to choke out.

"I saw you," he accused, "are you calling me a fuckin' liar?" The Frog loomed closer as if he were about to tongue a fly off my nose.

"No, sir!" I was the fuckin' liar, sir, I admitted to myself. It was me.

"Then why are you eyeballing me," he persisted. "You think I'm cute? You in love with me?"

"No, Sir," I screamed, absolutely truthfully.

"Then quit eye seducing me and get your eyes to the front!"

"You, broad," he challenged, turning to my neighbor turd, "what're you looking at? You inspecting my body? You think I came back here so you can rest your *hot beady eyes* on me? You goddammed sex maniac, get your eyes to the front!"

Why is he so obsessed with the thought of his imaginary good looks, I asked myself. Maybe because he really knows he is ugly as sin and he's trying to call attention to something else. If he didn't try so hard to socialize he might fit in better. Lord, spare me from this loony frog. Let me have the next DI. I'll go to church, I'll quit drinking beer, I won't go out with bad girls, I'll….

"Haven't I seen your face on a wanted poster," Froggy confronted another of my neighbors. "What's your seventh general order?"

"Sir, I don't know!"

"You don't *know*? Weren't you told to memorize the eleven general orders? You better damn well learn them before you meet your drill instructor. Or maybe," he put his hands together and cracked his knuckles, "you belong to me."

"What's your name, turd," Froggy grabbed the turd's Adam apple.

The turd struggled to speak, but could not.

"You're in trouble, turd. The questions get harder."

"When I call out your name, you will answer 'here, sir' in a loud clear voice." Froggy croaked off seventy-five names but Everett K. Joyce was spared, unless the count was contested.

"You turds whose names I called – *get outside*! Move out! Get out! Get out! Get out! You better not be last!"

Both DIs pushed, shoved, and dragged their prey out the door. Only when the last turd was assisted out by Froggy's foot did I breathe a sigh of relief.

A feeling of total dislike was building up for my laughing hometown recruiter. "Join the Marine Corps. The Marine Corps builds men."

Out of what? Turds? Girls? Cruds?

And if I were scared shitless, could I technically be called a turd? Three or four more hours of sitting at attention dragged by.

I recalled my send off at the recruiting station. Smiling Jack, our recruiting sergeant, herded us into a room to await an officer to swear us in.

"In a few minutes the Captain will be in to administer the oath to join the Marine Corps. You will then be in the Marines Corps but not a Marine. You are Marines *only* when you graduate from Parris Island. You have to *earn* the title. I'll give you a piece of advice: In your information packet is a sheet called General Orders for Sentries. I strongly advise you to memorize them before you get off the train at Yemassee, South Carolina. The Captain will be in shortly. Stand up straight, no talking, sound off loud and clear when you are taking the oath. Don't embarrass me, boys. Ten Hut!"

And the Captain walked in. We entered the Marine Corps without status and were immediately herded to the station and onto the first train heading south.

The General's Orders

Since we were silly civilian shits, we didn't bother to memorize the General Orders. Most recruits slept, played poker and shot the bull through Virginia and North Carolina.

Only those of us still awake in South Carolina thought to even look to see what the General Orders were about. It seemed a bit strange that the General was so worried about us that he took the trouble to address this item first.

I pulled my copy of the general orders out of my duffel bag and spread it on my desk. There were eleven.

The first seemed simple enough: "To take charge of this post and all government property in view." This really gave you a lot of authority. In a large installation you could probably see government property for a mile or so. I wondered if they had a soda fountain.

General Order Number 2: "To walk my post in a military manner, keeping always on the alert and observing everything that takes place within sight or hearing." Kind of like being a roving reporter.

General Order 3: "To report all violations of orders I am instructed to enforce." This sounded like a passive measure. Should I just watch someone violate or should I stop him from violating? Should I just let him go, or what? Why couldn't I just shoot him, or at least spray his feet with a few warning shots? Every sentry I had ever seen had a rifle; what was that for?

General Order 4: "To repeat all calls from posts more distant from the guardhouse than my own." I could call for backup.

General Order 5: "To quit my post only when properly relieved." I would punch the clock, no problem.

General Order 6: "To receive, obey, and pass on to the sentry who relieves me all orders from the Commanding General, Officer of the Day, and officers and non-commissioned officers of the guard only." This was a long one; I'd save it for later.

General Order 7: "To talk to no one except in the line of duty." A close mouthed bunch.

General Order 8. "To give the alarm in case of fire or disorder." I knew yelling "Fire! Fire!" was the right alarm for fire. Was yelling "Disorder! Disorder!" the right alarm for disorder?

General Order 9: "To call the Corporal of the Guard in any case not covered by instructions." What about the General? After all, they were *his* orders.

General Order 10: "To salute all officers and colors and standards not cased." What did a "cased officer" look like? I suppose the corporal would know. He could always kick it up to the general if he didn't.

General Order 11: "To be especially watchful at night and during the time for challenging, to challenge all persons on or near my post and to allow no one to pass without proper authority." Another long one I'd save for last.

My strategy was to study the shortest ones, like not talking to anyone and shouting disorder. My favorite one was taking charge. Maybe they'd give a multiple choice quiz.

All in all, I was in deep trouble and things didn't look any better going forward. There had to be a way to escape this situation.

Maybe I could contract a little leprosy, or the plague or something. Surely they'd have to send me home for a little period of recuperation. Then when they came for me, they'd have to pry my fingernails out of the back porch. Or maybe from an extended vacation to Canada. I wondered how extradition was these days.

Meeting Our DIs

"Standby, attention!" Chairs scraped, and seventy-five turds jackknifed to their feet. I almost fell out of my chair in my struggle to stand, my thoughts being somewhere between Canada and Parris Island, South Carolina. Two more Smokey Bears had arrived. They stood together, shaking their heads in disgust.

"Keerist," the short, bow-legged one with three stripes griped. "What shithole did they find these turds in? The recruiters must have shoveled shit for a year to get so many turds in the same room!"

"My name is Staff Sergeant Sword," the other Smokey Bear monotoned. He was a taller version of Montgomery Clift and his khaki uniform had creases on creases. "I am your Senior Drill Instructor. This is Sergeant Snake. Sound off when I call your name."

SSgt. Sword read off the names. No emotion or expression of any sort appeared on his face, compared with the wicked smiles and thunderclouds of his colleague. He had four stripes on his sleeves, three pointed up and one down.

"Izzakowski, Robert E.!"

"Here, Sir!"

"Jones, Bernard K.!"

"Here, Sir!"

"Jones, William T.!"

"Here, Sir!"

"Joyce, Everett K.!"

"Here, Sir," I screamed, feeling a wave of relief. At last! I belonged! In this miracle worker's hands rested my body, if not my soul, for the next twelve weeks. The good sergeant finished reading off the names.

"The turds whose names I just called are in Platoon 2037. You will pick up the black pen on your desk and write '2037' on the back of your left hand. Pick up your gear and get outside. On the double, *git*!"

"You heard the Senior Drill Instructor," Sergeant Snake threatened, "get your shit and get outside! I don't want to see anything but assholes and elbows! Move! Move! *Move!*"

The required swarm of assholes and elbows clawed madly for the door. Some elbows were partially dislocated by a sergeantly yank and some assholes received an occasional kick. My bag got caught between two turds' shoulders and I rode out of the building like a tin can on a cat's tail. I somehow arrived outside unscathed and was pushed into the eye of the mob.

Sgt. Snake was already outside, threatening and jerking latecomers out of the building. "You better get your ass out here, Granny! Come on, come on, line up, line up!"

Snake constantly squinted, like he was looking at a running deer over rifle sights. I've never seen a cobra face to face, but I know it would look exactly the same. He strutted with his arms held out from his sides, as though he was at any moment going to draw on us in a gunfight. His deep, mocking voice erupted from the bottom of his stomach, vomiting insults and orders.

"Pick up your bags! Who told you to put your bags down? What's the matter, you girls tired already? Stand up straight! Face to the right! Your *other* right, Numb One!" Snake screamed, punctuating his instruction with a jab to Numb One's stomach.

"Everybody hold up his right hand," SSgt. Sword instructed. "All right, this is the right. Remember it! Study it! When we say turn to the right, this is where we mean. All right, start walking! That's right, just fall all over yourselves! Didn't you even learn how to *walk* at home?"

I blindly followed the turd in front of me, my bag disagreeing every now and then, first pulling this way and then that, tripping me with every other step.

"Keep your eyes on the turd's head in front of you,"

SSgt. Sword droned, "you're not out on a picnic. Close it up! Get it closed up!"

The two drill instructors were all over the platoon, shoving and pushing, screaming all the while. Occasionally, they shoved a lagging turd so hard that several turds in front of him were pushed down to their knees. They scrambled along on their hands and knees until they could regain their feet.

My already bruised shins took the worst of it, closing up the two or three inches between them and my predecessor's heels. An occasional push from the turd behind didn't help much, either. The whole struggling centipede must have appeared fascinating to an onlooker, but it was sheer mass punishment to those of us who had the starring role. Arms flailing about, people tripping, bags flying, dozens of people half running, half walking, and all of us half blind and off balance.

Most of the time we couldn't see two feet in front of us. I supposed this was to keep us from remembering the way back. After an excruciating length of time, they told us to 'whoa.' We were in the middle of a street in front of a chow hall. Out of the corner of my eye, I could see other mobs of men. Their mobs were dressed in green and were in neat rectangles.

"A little while ago you learned which way was "right," SSgt. Sword reminded us. "Now we're going to turn to the "left." That's the other way. Let's all turn to the left – now! *No! No! No!* You lamebrains! Get back the way you were! We'll do it the way you learned."

"Turn to the right! Turn to the right! Turn to the right! Since you're not that advanced to understand what "left" is yet, we'll do everything to the right. We wouldn't want to overload your pea brains."

CHAPTER 3 – SETTLING IN

Sit, You Heathens

"We're going into the mess hall now," SSgt. Sword advised. "When you get into the hall, you'll get into line and take everything you want, but take only what you can eat. You will eat everything on your tray. The Marine Corps doesn't waste food. To see that you people don't waste our food, we post guards with billy clubs over the slop buckets on your way out."

Okay, clean your plate or get bludgeoned with a billy club. I could grasp that. After the morning cuisine, I wondered if I could identify the slop buckets. If it were SOS, it might be hard to tell.

"…will be eight men to a table." SSgt. Sword had been talking while I was daydreaming. "The eighth man will…"

A splash of bright red moving from my left caught my eye and I again went back to daydreaming. It seemed to be coming closer. Being a skirt watcher from way back, I sneaked a sideways glance. But it was only someone's cleaning lady or a female turd, perhaps.

"….will say 'ready seats.'" Sword was finishing, "then you will feed your faces as fast as you can and get back out here on the street. Right *here*. No talking, no moving around, just walking and eating. Is that clear?"

"Yes, sir!"

"Is *that clear*?"

"Yes, sir!"

We formed into two lines and filed into the chow

hall. I got into the right one, if that means anything. Staff Sgt. Sword supervised my line and pointed to the tables where we were to sit. Glancing up a couple of times, I saw the eighth man pick up a little card, read something and the eight men all sat down together, like a choir.

The way the food line worked was that you picked up a shiny aluminum tray with six compartments. Sidestepping your way down the food line, you held your tray out in front of you if you wanted each mess man to ladle whatever goody he was serving onto your tray. If you kept your tray in front of him, he'll keep giving you another goop until you pulled it back. I helped myself to some green beans, mashed potatoes, a shimmering wedge of orange gelatin and a chunk of unknown substance.

I turned to find SSgt. Sword urgently motioning me to a table and benches for eight. As I mentally counted the turds already standing at attention at their benches and those enroute, my heart sank as I realized I was the *eighth man*. Sitting my tray down on the table, not daring to look left or right for a clue as to what to do, I heard shouts of "Ready seats!" and "Our Lord thou who..." and "Ready, Seats!"

I carefully picked up a laminated prayer card under the watchful eye of SSgt. Sword. I studied it as long as I safely could, but he didn't seem to be hungry himself.

"Ready, seats," a turd near me shouted.

"Ready, seats," I boomed, and we all started to glide into our seats.

Whapp! A flash of green, accompanied by a stinging sensation on my left cheek, immediately distracted my attention from the chow. I was instantly aware and alert. I had screwed up. While I was thinking along these lines, I was being dragged to my feet and given the opportunity to learn from my mistakes.

For what we are about to receive we give thanks.
Photo courtesy of United States Marine Corps.

SSgt. Sword's face was so close to mine I leaned back. He kept coming. "You stupid dipshit," he growled, the vein in his neck pulsing, "I told you to read the prayer *first*! Everybody up! Now read it!"

I chose the shortest prayer, quickly read it and meekly ordered "ready seats." If the meek truly do inherit the earth, his ass might be the first one we kick off. I faked an intense interest in my chow, my tray and the table in front of me, until SSgt. Sword slowly shook his head and moved toward the next table.

Didn't these people know about the "personal comfort zone?" You weren't supposed to get closer than twelve inches to someone unless you were going to kiss them. Every time Sword and Snake got in my face for the first three weeks it scared the bejesus out of me. Sure, they knew, it was in their handbook: "Twenty Ways to Scare the Bejesus out of Civilians."

Putting On the Right Face

After chow, we ran out to the street and lined up as ordered. SSgt. Sword and Sgt. Snake came out of their part of the mess hall and stomped around, counting turds. A few heavy eaters came running, wiping their mouths with their sleeves, and sneaking into line.

"Well, no shit, you goddammed gluttons," Sgt. Snake screamed, "did you leave anything for anyone else? You think we enjoy standing around out here while you're in there stuffing yourselves? You people will be out here and waiting before we exit the mess hall! Don't be the last one out next time!"

Snake stuck his chin in the face of a fragile-looking black recruit. "Is the gang all here now, Buckwheat?" Without waiting for an answer, he turned abruptly and marched to the rear of the herd.

"Okay, turds," yelled SSgt. Sword, "I'm going to give the order for 'right face.' Everyone hold up his right hand!"

"This *one*, Numb One! That's right. When I say 'right, face' everyone will turn to his right. When I say 'right,' no one does anything. When I then say 'face' you will come out of your daze and actually turn to the right."

"I will demonstrate for you college people. Everyone watch my feet. On 'right' I don't do anything, but I know I am getting ready to do something. On 'face,' I pivot on the ball of my left foot and the heel of my right. Then I bring my left foot up alongside and click the heel of my right foot, like this."

Sgt. Sword executed the maneuver smartly, his heels singing out like a pistol shot.

"I'll do it once more." He crooked his finger at the nearest recruit. "You, Stooge, get out here."

The unfortunate stooge lumbered out to the drill instructor and stood facing him at rigid attention.

"Well, turn *around*, Stooge," SSgt. Sword directed with a shove, "I already know how to do it; they don't. When I give the word, we'll do it together. All right. With me now, right - face!"

Our stooge turned stiffly, catching his left toe on the heel of his right shoe. He fell against SSgt. Sword, who caught him by his shoulder and propelled him into our bungling midst.

"Oh, that was *outfuckingstanding*, Swivelhips! I'll bet they got *lots* more like you at home." Sword turned, and walked away, disgusted. Just when I thought he had given up on us, he glanced at the sky, shook his head, and walked slowly back to the platoon.

"All right, when I give the order, you'll all stumble around to the right. That's the direction your right hand's on. Block everything out of your pea brains except the words 'turn to the right!' Later on, maybe we'll learn how Marines do it. Get your feet together! Stand up straight! Now listen up! Turn to the right!"

We managed to elbow our way around to the right in which no one was knocked to the ground. I thought we did quite well.

"Oh, beautiful girls," Sgt. Snake agreed, "that was goddammed wonderful! It's too bad we've only got twelve weeks to get it right. But we can learn. Can't we, girls? I said *can't we?*"

"Yes, sir," we shouted.

"I can't hear you!"

""Yes, sir," we yelled

"Louder!"

"Yes, sir," we screamed. This shit was giving me a headache.

"You people are without a doubt the sorry assed bunch of turds ever to hit this island," Sgt. Snake lamented. "You shitbirds are lower than whale shit! And you know where that is? It's at the bottom of the goddammed ocean! You people wouldn't even make a pimple on a Marine's ass! Bunch of women."

So I was consorting with persons lower than whaleshit and other lowlife. There goes the fucking neighborhood. Yes, my language had already degenerated into that of a foul mouthed sailor. After all my mornings in Sunday school; all of the hours under the tutelage of the sharp noses of English teachers. Rotten pricks will do that to you.

Sgt. Snake looked over to SSgt. Sword, who seemed busy trying not to notice us.

"All right, girls," the silver tongued Snake bellowed, "let's all skip down to that building down the road. Fooorrrwaard Ho!"

Let Them Wear Skivvies

They herded us along for a few hundred yards, constantly screaming insults about our lack of coordination and alleged composition of our heads. Then we stopped, did our one and only military maneuver, and stood hopefully awaiting our next meal.

Instead, we filed into a one-story steel shed filled with rows of bins. Each bin contained a sheet of brown wrapping paper, some cord and a pencil.

"You will take everything off and wrap it in the paper in the bin. You will take everything out of your wallet and spread it across the bin! You will deposit all condoms and dirty pictures in the GI can!"

"If you are wearing an expensive watch, you will send it home. If you are wearing a cheap watch you may keep it. You people don't need a watch anyway. We will tell you when it's time to eat, shit, or go blind!"

"Therefore, the only things you will end up with are a wallet, a cheap watch, and a ring if you are married. Everything else goes! Tennis rackets, sunglasses, suntan oil, teddy bears, hair rollers, ukuleles, everything! When you are finished, place the package on the conveyer belt. Get hot!"

I stripped down to my altogether and threw my clothes, shoes and watch in my bag. I wrapped the bag in the paper, tied it with string, and addressed to my mother. As I dropped it onto the conveyer, I felt like I had lost my identity, which I guess I had.

I now had nothing to do. What do you do when you're standing buck-naked, except for goose bumps, in a room with seventy-four other naked guys without anything to wear and no place to go? Most of these guys looked up at the rafters, at the walls; just about any place except each other.

"Everybody got their zoot suits on the conveyer," SSgt. inquired. "You will carry your wallet in your mouth! Line up in two files and follow me. Come on, Tarzan, nobody's looking at your skinny ass!"

The lines were fed into the shavers of two barbers. I lost every hair down to the scalp in five or six sweeps. My barber, probably a former Australian sheep shearer, seemed a little disappointed with my sparse mop as I normally wore a crew cut. Nevertheless, he did a fine job altering the natural curvature of my skull.

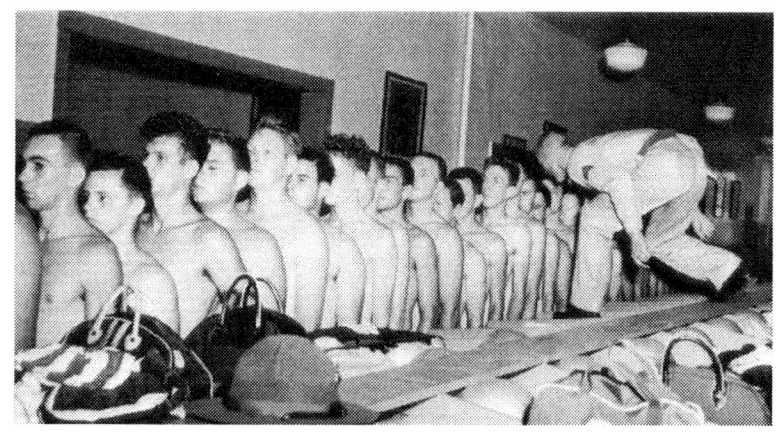

A drill instructor "encourages" recruits to keep their eyeballs to the front. Photo courtesy of United States Marine Corps.

With our skinhead haircuts my fellow turds and I now resembled a horde of nude Tibetan Monks.

I followed the rest of the skinheads into a tiled room where three jolly green giants beat the crap out of us with thick Turkish towels. I think the idea was to knock off the hair left from the barbers, but I swear they removed some that was still growing.

Then into the shower room, where Sgt. Snake stood by to make sure that we washed behind our ears.

From there we were funneled into a sort of adjoining clothing warehouse. They threw you a seabag, then you stepped in front of a window and shouted your waist size. Size 30 got you a size 32; size 38 got you a size 32, and so on. You had to be quick, because admitting a size immediately got you several flying pairs of shorts and T-shirts.

We put on a pair of shorts and a T-shirt to ward off a possible attack by love starved female Marines, which appeared a bit scarce, but you never know.

When we had gone through the socks, trouser, shirt

and shoe windows, I had a bulging seabag that I couldn't even lift. I managed to find the strength when Snake slithered over, hands on hips, demanding, "You waiting for a smoking jacket, turd? Pick up your bag and get your ass outside!"

For the first time, our herd was dressed in all the same color: green. We now wore green trousers, definitely not "pants" as we were advised only women wore pants, and shirts with white tags still attached, called "utilities." A soft green cap with a brim, called a "cover" completed the ensemble. Almost nothing was called by its regular name, including shorts. They were called "skivvies."

I had to roll up the bottoms of my trousers a couple of times. Either I was too short for the waist size or they expected me to grow a couple of inches.

Home, Sweet Home

"We're goin' home now, Kiddies," SSgt. Sword said, "pick up your bag and put it on your right shoulder! Pick it up! Get it up there! Turn to the right! Move out. Pick up that bag, turd! Keep it closed up! Get moving!"

We stumbled, dragged and manhandled the seabags and ourselves down several streets, arriving in front of a 2-story white frame building.

"Whoa, mob! Stop," Snake screamed as we struggled to stop the momentum of the heavy seabags surging forward. "Put your bag down! Right face! That means the barracks is in *front* of you, Numb One! Turn around!"

Snake walked over to the barracks entrance and held the door open. I thought it very courteous of him, until I thought of the spider and the fly.

"When I give the word," SSgt. Sword ordered, "you

will get in the barracks and into the squadbay. Put your seabag on a rack and stand at attention in front of your rack. Alright, get inside!"

The horde scrambled toward the building, clawing to get inside all at once with their seabags. Sword and Snake stepped into the melee, pushing, shoving, and screaming "hurry up, hurry up!"

We arrived in a rectangular room with forty or so double decker racks, three or four rifle racks and a large garbage can. Glancing around, I saw no pictures on the wall, no curtains, no lamps, or furniture. A real opulent sort of place.

"You people are at '*attention,*'" Snake screamed, "you just don't fall all over yourselves as soon as you stop walking! You will stand at attention, sit at attention, shit at attention, and you will lie at attention in your racks! Do you understand?"

"Yes, sir," we screamed back. Did that mean we couldn't roll over in our racks, or was there a horizontal side position of attention?

"Get at attention," Snake screamed. "That means your heels are together, your feet are at a 45 degree angle! Your arms are at your side, elbows in, with your thumbs along your trouser seams! Your fingers are curled and touching your trouser leg. Stand up straight! Look straight ahead! Suck it in!"

No wonder people can't learn to play golf.

"You may have heard of 'at ease,'" Snake went on, "but it *doesn't exist* for you people!" I guess that means my afternoon nap during "Howdy Doody Time" is out of the question too?

"You people are Platoon 2037," Sword rasped, "one of four platoons in India Company. Three other companies, Fox, Golf, and Hotel make up the Second Battalion. Sgt.

Snake will give you your address tonight when you write letters home!"

I wondered if the accommodations were any better in Hotel Company. Or whether the days were more carefree in Golf?

"When Sgt. Snake calls your name you will answer up 'Here, Sir,'" SSgt. Sword bellowed. "When I touch your shoulder, you will take one step forward!"

Sgt. Snake called out the names while SSgt. Sword walked along the racks, choosing six of the tallest turds.

After Snake was satisfied that none had escaped, Sword returned to the first rack in line. He walked along the bunks, counting.

"One, two, three, four, five, six, seven, eight, nine, ten, eleven, twelve! You people are in the first squad."

Sword walked to the nearest tall turd and grabbed him by the shoulder. "What did you do before they ran out of food back home, Tiny?"

"Sir, I..." Tiny began.

"You don't say 'I' here, turd," Sword growled, "you don't say 'me' and you don't say 'you!' You will refer to yourself as 'the private' or 'Private Tiny!' You will refer to the drill instructor as the 'drill instructor!' For example, 'Sir, the private was a member of a street gang.'"

I, too, was one for not becoming overly familiar at this early stage. I barely *knew* these guys. It appeared that the drill instructors could say the forbidden words, however. The rules didn't apply to them. They could say, for example, "I'll kick your ass" and we weren't supposed to be offended by their damn overly familiar terms.

"You will not speak unless you are spoken to! On those rare occasions in which you absolutely have to make a head call, or you notice we are being invaded, you will sound off, loud and clear, 'Sir, Private Turd requests permission to speak to the drill instructor!' Then, with the drill instructor's permission you will state your request."

Sort of like requesting permission to request permission.

"Well," SSgt. Sword resumed, facing Tiny again, "what did you do?"

"Sir, the private was a student at the University of Northern Kentucky," Tiny proclaimed proudly.

"I'm fucking *thrilled* to hear it. Jesus, a goddammed *college* boy! Are you a *leader*?"

"Sir," Tiny bragged, "the private was *Captain* of the football team!"

"You oughta be in good shape, then. Get down and give me twenty pushups!"

"You," he pointed at the next tallest turd, "what do you do?"

"Sir, the private worked in a tannery! The private was a hide trimmer, Sir!"

"Are you telling me you cut assholes out of bull hides?"

"Yes, sir!"

"Sounds like good experience to me. From now on you will tear new assholes out of turds. You're the first squad leader! Grab your seabag and move it here," Sword said, pointing to the first rack.

"Move your shit down a rack," he pointed to the College Boy.

He walked the length of the squadbay, counting off squads and putting the tallest turds in charge as squad leaders. Being only 5 foot 8, I had no leadership potential, and ended up in the last and shortest squad.

One remaining tall turd was assigned "section leader" in charge of the squad leaders and all us common turds. Sort of like "King of the Turds."

"You squad leaders will shape up all the turds in your squads. If they need help in marching, squaring away their gear, doing pushups, you will make sure they do it right."

"Every time they fuck up, *you* fuck up! Every time they have to do pushups, *you* have to do pushups! So does the section leader!"

That didn't sound so great. Maybe I wasn't meant to be a leader, after all.

Shopping Spree

After all the brown noses got promoted, SSgt. Sword gave the word to get outside.

"Hurry up! Move it! Move! Move! You better not be last, turd! We have things to do, girls!"

Once I had seen a movie, in which a cheetah cut out the smallest, weakest gazelle of the herd, ran it down and grabbed it by the neck. The herd of gazelles paced nervously before the attack, keeping an eye on the cheetah. I felt kinship with the gazelles. I tried to stay in the eye of the herd and never to be on the outer rank.

After all of the turds were flushed back outside and reassembled, SSgt. Sword tried again with the right face.

"You people are at 'attention!' Stand up straight! Suck in that gut!" Sword gave a short rabbit punch to the gut of the offending turd. "Lift up your chest! Get your eyes to the front! Right," he paused, "face!"

"Jesus Christ," he muttered as most of us twisted to the right. Although he wasn't pleased, I could see improvement there.

"We are now going to try to march again. When I say 'forward', you will wait until I say 'march', then you will step off with your left foot! When I say 'left' you will put your left foot down and when I say 'right' you will put your right foot down! This is called cadence. I will call cadence only when necessary, which for you turds will probably be all the time!"

"Forward," he paused, "march! Left, right, left, right! Get with it, Numb Nuts! Left, right, left, right! Goddamm it, turd, listen up!"

We left-righted it down several streets and stopped in front of another one story white building that looked like a general store. It was. A wooden sign identified it as the Triangle PX.

"When you walk through the hatch, you will take a white laundry bag from the shelf on your left and a list from the table. You will get everything on the list. You will not pick up anything not on the list. Do you understand?"

"Yes, sir!"

"If you are a smoker, you may buy one carton of cigarettes. If you are a non-smoker, you won't buy cigarettes. That is the only exception!"

What about cigars? I had once worked at the tobacco counter in a drugstore and the druggist said I could have any cigar as long as I smoked it. He lost money on that deal, because I came to enjoy Garcia y Vega Presidentes and smoked plenty of them.

"When the list says buy three toothbrushes, you *will* buy three toothbrushes. No magazines, no souvenirs, no candy. No alcoholic after-shave. Do you understand?"

"Yes, sir," we screamed. But what about cigars? Since we had no money, the PX was apparently going to let us run a tab.

We filed through the PX, collecting items on the list,

shaving cream, razors, writing paper, two padlocks, a can of Brasso, toothpaste, and the required three toothbrushes. No soft drinks, chewing gum, paperback novels, or cigars. Only the Spartan necessities for building men.

After left-righting it back home, we dumped our treasures onto our bunks so that the drill instructors could verify our purchases. This went pretty much without incident, except for two turds; one that missed purchasing toothpaste, the other razor blades.

The turd that missed buying razor blades was the second squad leader.

"Didn't I just make you a squad leader," Sword demanded.

"Yes, sir!"

"Well, you're fired," Sword growled. "how in the hell can you tell other turds what to do when you can't follow simple instructions? You, turd," he grabbed another large turd, "you're second squad leader now!"

"On the deck beneath the bottom racks are two wooden locker boxes! You will place everything except your empty laundry bag and one towel into the box. You will neatly lay all clothing and your folded up seabag on the bottom of the box. You will put all your 'smell goods' in the top tray."

"You will lock the box with one of your locks. Tie your laundry bag on the rear of your rack opposite your towel. That's where your dirty clothes will go, not on the floor or on your rack like you did at home!"

After chow, Sword had us stand in front of our racks and count off to make sure we didn't lose anyone to food poisoning.

"Take a look at the turds around you. Some of you won't be here this time tomorrow. Those of you who are too fat, too salty, or too puny to cut it here will be gone. We have a Fat Man's Platoon for you fat asses, a Motivation Platoon for you badasses, and a funny farm for you babies that can't hack it."

He then had us make up our racks the way Sgt. O'Brien had instructed. The racks failed inspection two times before Sword lost his patience.

"Get down for pushups! On my count, *one*!"

We struggled to hold our bodies off the deck as Sword and Snake walked along the racks, stepping between bodies.

"Two! Three! Four!"

"Get your knees off the floor, Lard Ass," Snake screamed at a heavy recruit, "we don't do them like the girls do!"

Lard Ass struggled to raise his chest from the floor.

"Get your tits off the floor, Elsie! What're you – about a 38-B cup? Were you breast fed for twenty years?" I hoped Lard Ass knew Snake was still talking to him. It was hard to keep track of who was who.

Lard Ass tried mightily, but succeeded only in making a rocking motion.

"I didn't say roll back and forth, Jelly Belly," Snake bellowed. "Lift your fat ass off the deck! You are a goddammed 'blivik', Jelly Belly! Do you know what a blivik is?"

"No, sir!"

"A blivik is ten pounds of shit in a five pound bag! We have a special platoon for bliviks and fat asses. Tomorrow we go to the dispensary to separate the fat asses from the candy asses. You'll probably get the opportunity to train a couple of extra weeks with your fellow fat asses in the Fat Man's Platoon."

We understood Lard Ass, a.k.a. Elsie, a.k.a. Jelly Belly the Blivik, would probably be on his way to the Fat Man's Platoon tomorrow.

After completing fifteen or twenty pushups, we were given a chance to make up the racks again. This time SSgt. Sword grudgingly accepted them. At least we had no mattress walk and he didn't seem to have a three-year-old kid.

Sword inspected all the racks. Finding a good one, he turned to Private Sterling. "Is this your rack?"

"Sir, yes, sir."

"You are now 'House Mouse.' Report to my hatch when we are done here."

SSgt. Sword conferred briefly with Sgt. Snake and left, apparently having given up on us for the rest of the day. We were now in the hands of the Snake.

Letters to Mommy

"Open your locker boxes and get out your marking materials. You should have a marking stamp with your name on it, a name tag, black ink and a roll of white tape. You will stamp your name on your skivvies, T-shirts and utility trousers, blouses, and covers. Stamp your name on pieces of tape and put them on your socks. Stamp the name tag and button it on your utility blouse."

We spent two hours stamping our new clothing under Snake's supervision. Finally we had our wardrobe personalized, folded, and stowed away.

"Open your locker boxes and get out your writing material." Sgt Snake ordered. "We are going to write Mommy and let her know you heroes have arrived safely at Parris Island so she doesn't worry."

"You will *not* write your girl friend, your fan club, or

the society page of your local newspaper! It *will be* to your mommy if you have one, otherwise to your father or your grandmother or whoever you lived with."

I was tempted to write "Wild Thing," a girl I had started to date a month before leaving for Parris Island. I brought Wild Thing home for dinner once, in which Martha and Everett's baby boy got the fisheye from Mom and an approving stare from Dad. Maybe if I put *Mrs.* Wild Thing and claimed she was my stepmother... No, I was half afraid even to write my own *mother*. Wild Thing would have to wait.

"Okay," he continued, "write this down: 'Dear Mommy. I have arrived at Parris Island. It is really a nice place and I'm excited to start my training. My drill instructor is a nice guy. We call him 'Sarge.'"

"The first turd to call me 'Sarge,'" Snake interrupted himself, "will be the *last* one to call me 'Sarge.' No, don't write that down, you dimwits!"

"And I'm *not* a nice guy," he went on, "but that's the kind of bullshit that these people will eat up and they'll sleep better knowing their Little Skip or Chip or Sonny is down here having a big tea party."

After quoting the address where our mommies were to write us, he told us to advise our mommies that they or anyone else were not to send us cookies or candy as our diet would be strictly regulated. And that we did not need, or deserve, "pogey bait" anyway.

"All right, you turds got all that?"

"Yes, Sir!"

"All right, we need a nice homey finish. O.K. Put this down, 'Well, I have to go now as Sarge is calling me to play softball.' And close 'Love, Turd or whatever your name is.' You will address your envelope but not seal it."

"You, turd," he pointed to the nearest turd; "collect

the letters and bring them to my hatch."

"Aye, Aye, Sir," Turd responded.

"When you approach my hatch, you will stand at attention outside the hatch and knock three times on the frame. When I say 'enter,' you will center your ass in the hatchway and sound off 'Private Turd reporting to the drill instructor as ordered, sir.' Do you understand?"

"Yes, sir!"

"Do all of you turds understand?"

"Yes, sir," we bellowed.

"When I say '2037,' you will all sound off 'platoon 2037' loud and clear! If I pass the word to get outside, you will all repeat '2037, get outside.' Do you understand?"

"Yes, sir!"

"It is now 2145 hours. That's a quarter till ten for you civilian pukes. The little hand is on ten and the big hand is on nine. In fifteen minutes, we will have lights out and hit the sack. One turd to a rack. To ensure that we don't go visiting after lights off, we will have a 'fire watch' on patrol."

"The fire watch will watch for fires, flashlights under the blankets, two turds in one rack, and anything else out of the ordinary."

"Ajax, Archibald, Baker and Brown," he read from his clipboard, "will be the first fire watch! You people report to my hatch for instructions after I'm done here."

"Aye, Aye, sir," they chorused.

"When reveille goes at 0500, you will get out of your racks and stand at attention at the foot of your racks with your sheets and blanket in your hands."

He consulted his watch. "You people have ten minutes to shit, brush your teeth, and square away your gear." He turned and left the squadbay.

"Aye, aye, sir! Standby, Attention!"

We turned to, shitting, brushing and writing.

"Private Tweeter," Snake yelled from his hut.

"Private Tweeter," we shouted.

"Get your ass in here," Snake finished.

"Get your ass in there," we echoed.

Snake instantly appeared in the hatchway, hands on hips.

"Standby, attention," we screamed.

"*I'm the one* to say 'get your ass in here,'" Snake corrected, "you people say 'Private Tweeter, report to the drill instructor'! Is that clear?"

"Yes, Sir!"

"You people have *shit* for brains!"

Turning on his heel, Snake stalked away, muttering. We didn't repeat whatever he said.

Except for the half hour nap the first night, we had been up for over thirty-eight hours. I think that nap made us feel worse, not better. It was hard to believe that less than forty-eight hours ago I had been a fat, dumb, and happy silly civilian shit.

I wondered what the heck I was doing in Parris Island. I realize that signing on the dotted line had something to do with it, but what made me do that? True, the economy was not good in the summer of 1958, and I couldn't even get my old job back at the grocery store after attending college for six months. Living at home while unemployed in those days was considered abnormal.

Plus, my father was from the old "German School." While he didn't blow a whistle and line us up like O'Brien's kids, he was very outspoken and had definite ideas about what my brother and I should do or be doing. Heck, he was dominating. I thought maybe the Marine Corps could turn me into someone who could debate him.

I started school when I was five and skipped a grade. Therefore I was two years younger than my classmates and generally was considered a younger brother or mascot, rather than an equal. So after graduating high school I pumped gas, worked in a grocery store, and waited for my sophomore girlfriends to graduate.

That brings me back to Wild Thing. She was one of my sophomore friends and I could lord it over her that I was six days older than she. We didn't have a single thing in common but she was very cute and sexy. Dad liked her very much but my mother thought she shouldn't come to dinner anymore.

That's why I joined the Marine Corps. Doesn't sound like much of a reason, whatever it was, but I was hoping *you* could see the logic. Maybe I was foolish enough to want to beard the lion in his den and measure myself by my own yardstick. Well, that's neither here nor now, because I was there then, gainfully employed bearding lions at thirteen cents an hour. At least they paid me while I slept.

CHAPTER 4 – TESTING, 1, 2

Turn and Cough

A tremendous crash jarred me out of a deep sleep. I opened my eyes to see a 50-gallon metal garbage can careening off bunks, finally coming to rest against one of the rifle racks. What sounded like a full orchestra started to blast reveille on the street outside our barracks. It seemed clear that reveille was going to cause a commotion every morning.

Our day started with bright lights, yelling and a flurry of activity. The lights of the barracks on both sides went on simultaneously and the screams of drill instructors, men chanting orders in unison, and pounding feet filled the air. The only things missing were the wail of air raid sirens and the frantic passing out of gas masks.

I bounded out of my rack, grabbed the sheets and blanket, and froze at attention at the front of the rack. I swayed, half awake as the band thundered on. Sgt Snake strutted into the room.

"Standby, attention," we shouted.

Snake strode quickly over to a turd, who had incredibly slept through it all, lifted the end of his rack and shook it until the sleeping turd spilled out and onto the deck.

"Get your ass outa the rack. Get your sheets in your hands!"

To Snake's immense delight, the half-awake turd walked into the wall. "Outstanding, Numb One," he chortled as he jerked the turd away from the wall and spun him around. The sleepy turd grabbed his sheets and blanket and froze in front of his rack.

"When I come in this squadbay tomorrow morning, all of you will be standing at attention in front of your rack with your sheets and blankets. That means the fire watch will wake each of you before reveille goes. Is that understood?"

"Yes, sir!"

Kind of like a two minute warning on reveille. Jimmy Dorsey and his cohorts mercifully finished playing.

"You people have thirty minutes to shit, shower and shave. You shit pumpers will shit between 0500 and 0530 or between 2130 and 2200 each day. You will shit how much I say, when I say and what color." Snake consulted his watch. "You will be standing in front of your racks dressed in utilities in twenty-eight minutes."

We spent most of the morning at the dispensary, getting checked out with medical and dental exams. Shots were administered on an assembly line basis, recruits sometimes getting shots in both arms at the same time. I got so many holes in my arms I occasionally checked to see if I was leaking somewhere.

We stood nude, our faces turned to the left while a doctor grabbed our wedding tackle and told us to cough.

We bent over and spread our cheeks while some perverse quack looked God knows where. We were jabbed, probed, X-rayed, and questioned until finally they were satisfied we could march without having a heart attack or spreading the Plague to our fellow turds.

We lost several turds because of consumption, jungle rot or simply being too fat. If you were overweight and could not get down to the required weight in twelve weeks, you were "set back" to the "fat man's platoon." There, they shrunk the fat men into semi-fat turds who could finish the job with a later platoon. As expected, Lard Ass, a.k.a. Elsie, a.k.a. Jelly Belly the Blivik, did not make the cut and was banished to the Fat Man's Platoon.

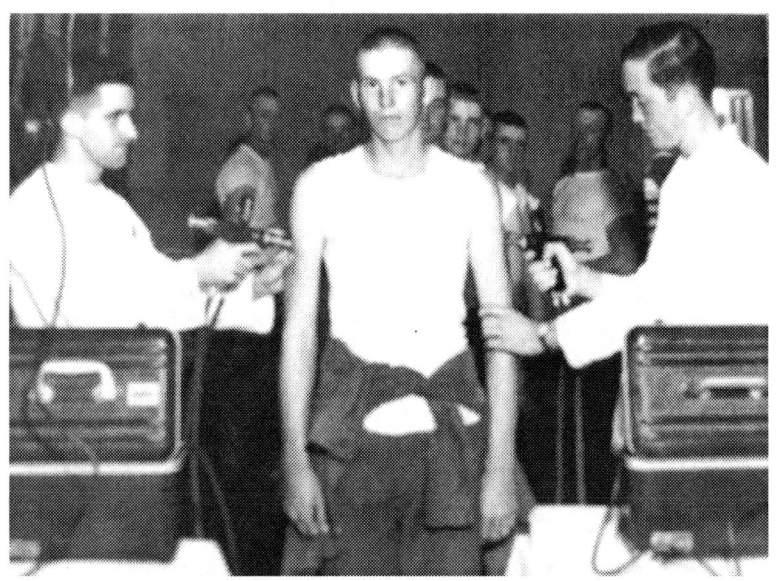

This recruit seems to be eyeing the two corpsmen
ahead of him with two more shots.
Photo courtesy of United States Marine Corps.

Others got a pink sheet that said they had to go back to the dispensary for dental fillings, eyeglasses or other appliances to correct their medical shortcomings. Since this meant the turds had to miss some training, the drill instructors were generally pissed off. I was stamped a healthy specimen and was spared for once.

Make a Muscle

We then went to an indoor gym for our "initial strength test." In this test we had to pass a minimum number of pull-ups, sit-ups, and other exercises to determine if there was any hope that we might complete the training in twelve weeks.

Half of the platoon assumed the pushup position while the other half lay on their stomachs and placed their hand on the deck to make sure our stomachs touched the ground, thereby doing an official pushup. My partner was Private Weezil who looked expectantly at the drill instructor each time my stomach barely touched his hand. I let myself down hard enough to crush his hand against the cement a few times to help keep his mind on counting, rather than unofficially evaluating my performance for the DI.

The serious recruit with the glasses could be Weezil.
Photo courtesy of United States Marine Corps.

    A few turds were too short to reach or jump up to the chin up bar and had to be lifted up to it by taller turds. The DIs let them hang there kicking for awhile; maybe hoping the exercise would stretch them a little. One turd almost managed to get his knees over the bar but couldn't get his chin to cooperate. Another's body went completely horizontal.

    Sword came over to him and pressed his hand down on the turd's rigid stomach. "How're you doing that, turd," he asked, mystified.

    Several turds couldn't do even one chin-up.

    "Those turds that can't do at least three chin-ups will be sent back to another platoon," SSgt. Sword advised. "Instead of being here twelve weeks, your stay will be extended another two or three weeks."

Several of the non-performing turds managed to do a chin up or two after this new inspiration.

Sgt. Snake carried his own version of inspiration called a "swagger stick," a polished wooden rod with a shell casing on one end and a bullet on the other. He tucked it under his arm and strutted around like Field Marshall Montgomery. In a moment of disappointment, he would whirl the stick out and zap a turd on the butt who then responded with a burst of energy up and over the bar. Halfway through the strength test I noticed he didn't have it anymore. I think SSgt. Sword took the stick away from him after seeing how much the would-be Field Marshall enjoyed using it.

They kept exact records of the number of pushups, sit-ups, chin-ups and other physical abuse requirements we could perform before they started to train us in earnest. But alas, the two or three who couldn't manage three chin ups were condemned to extend their stay in a conditioning platoon. Lard Ass would have definitely failed this if he hadn't already got the chop.

Let's Take a Dip

After noon chow, Snake gave us "the word."

"You will get dressed in your PT uniform, tennis shoes and socks! You will wear a jock strap whether you need one or not! You will be ready to fall outside with a towel in your hand in ten minutes!"

We tore off our new green utilities and struggled into our jock straps. I felt they had given me a "small", as some of the other smaller turds were able to pull theirs on up to their armpits. I wouldn't trade mine for their secondhand jock strap after that. The PT uniforms were neat, red shorts and gold shirts, emblazoned with "USMC" in red letters. Almost like we were members of a college track team. Turdeville U.

"Get outside!" I grabbed my towel and clocked my best time outside.

We were transported by bus to a large indoor swimming pool. At last, some recreation. A swimming party! Who said boot camp was all work and no play?

"You people form a line at the diving board! Hurry up! Move! No, we're not going to take time to skip stones! Move it!"

Shit, I thought, we're even going to swim by the numbers. No party. We were marched like lemmings over to the high diving board and up the ladder.

Two swimming instructors were treading water on either side of the board and another stood under the board, holding a long pole with a hook on it.

"Jump," the instructor ordered the first turd on the board.

The turd jumped, surfaced and swam back to the edge of the pool. He was then directed off the low diving board and swam to the far end of the pool and back for the rest of his test. He was then allowed to towel off and put on his shirt. Obviously, a winner. One by one my fellow turds jumped, swam, and got dressed. Until one turd shrank back from the diving board steps.

"Sir, this private can't swim," he shouted.

"Get up there," the instructor ordered.

"Sir, but this private can't swim," the turd pleaded.

"You heard the swimming instructor, turd! Get your ass up there," Sgt. Snake echoed, striding toward the ladder.

The turd shot up the ladder as Snake approached and stood frozen, his eyes fixed on the water.

"Sir, this private..." he started.

Snake started up the ladder.

"Sir, this...."

"Are you disobeying a direct order," Snake screamed, nearing the top of the ladder.

"Sir...."

"Get your ass off there!"

The turd moved quickly to the end of the board, looked back at the approaching Snake and stepped off.

"Yes, sirrrrrrrrrrr," he screamed on the way down.

Splash! Well, the turd was right. He sank like a plunging roller coaster. The two lifeguards swam down, grabbed him, and hauled him over to the edge.

"You're in the Esther Williams Class," Snake advised, "get over there," he pointed to an area along the edge, "and wait for your sisters!"

The swimming test continued, with turds jumping off, pushed off, or thrown off the diving board by Sgt. Snake. Those that sank like roller coasters were fished out with the hook and signed up for the Williams Class. One other turd, which churned the water in a circle like a bumblebee but made little or no forward progress, was also condemned to the class.

The turd in front of me was confident. He walked quickly to the end of the board, bounced, and did a "cannonball." He swam easily back to the edge, alternately backstroking and free styling like an Olympian.

"You, Johnny Weissmueller," Snake leaned over the edge, pointing at our Olympian. "you think you're some kind of goddammed *tuna*? Give me five laps around the pool to cool off your fins!"

Although I had been swimming since I was five, I quickly abandoned my plans to be the first to dive and then flash cleanly back to the edge. I stepped off, surfaced and doggy paddled strongly back to the edge. It was fairly easy, once you got clear of the guy with the hook.

Let's see if you can swim, turd.
Photo courtesy of United States Marine Corps.

After we had all taken our dips, the swimming instructor called us over for a huddle.

"Someday you may have to exit a sinking ship! It would be a mistake to think the damned Swabbies will always get you where you going! Neither can you wait till the damn thing sinks down to a convenient level where you can just step off into the water! Every Marine will know how to swim!"

You're In the Infantry, Turd

After our refreshing swim, we met Sgt. Gibson, our third and final drill instructor. A tall, raw-boned sort that looked as though he would have been at home either stampeding cattle or fighting alligators. I immediately labeled him "Hoot." At first glance, he didn't seem sadistic enough to be a drill instructor, but he quickly clarified things.

"My name's Sgt. Gibson and I'm the toughest sonofabitch on this island!"

Gee, I thought, *two* toughest sonofabitches. I wondered if he and Sgt. O'Brien knew about each other. Both being sonofabitches, they might even be related.

"You, Pilgrim," Hoot asked the nearest recruit, "what's your name?"

"Sir, the recruit's name is Private Hightower!"

"Hightower," Hoot mused, "you a fuckin' Indian?"

"No, sir."

"Sounds like a fuckin' Indian to me. You wouldn't be shittin' me, would you?"

"No, sir!"

"Well, *I* say you're a fuckin' Indian. You should be proud of your heritage, not like some fuckin' foreigner. This is your last chance. Now, Chief, are you a fuckin' Indian or not?"

"Sir," the newly christened Indian admitted, "the private is a fuckin' Indian if the drill instructor says so!"

"Okay, that's better. I *knew* you were a fuckin' Indian. Get down and give me *twenty* for lying!"

I was standing close enough to Hightower that Hoot could read my nametag. "Joyce," he taunted, "what the hell kinda name is that? "You a little girl?" You scribble little poems about trees?"

"No, *sir,*" I screamed in my deepest voice. I had expected this, having been through similar challenges over my eighteen years. I wanted to tell him that the surname "Joyce" was derived a Latinized form of Breton, meaning "Josse," or "lord," and that James Joyce the author never minded. But Hoot was already moving to the next turd.

We also meet Corporal Winston. Winston was the shortest, ugliest, out-of-shape Marine we had seen so far. He had short gray hair, a gut that stretched his starched khaki uniform and he slobbered and snorted as he waddled through the ranks.

Corporal Winston was an English bulldog.

"This here's Corporal Winston," Gibson declared as Winston lumbered over to Gibson and stood growling at the herd.

"Corporal Winston is a non-commissioned officer in these United States Marine Corps and as such, is entitled to every military courtesy. He outranks every turd in this platoon. Therefore, you will call him 'sir' on sight and will wish him 'good morning' or 'good afternoon' as the case may be."

"The Corporal is particularly sensitive to military courtesy and you will remember to call him 'sir.' Because if he *doesn't hear that*, he's liable to take a bite right out of your ass or lift his leg and piss on your shoe."

"Corporal Winston is the third of his line," Hoot

continued, "his original name was 'Marine' because if he isn't fightin' or fuckin', he's sitting on his ass bitchin'. You would do well to keep out of his way."

As if to prove Hoot's point, Winston broke formation and galloped across the street where a large black mongrel was urinating on a pole supporting a steam pipe. Spying the onrushing Winston, the mongrel abruptly stopped watering the pole, and ran hell bent for leather up the street, growling back over his shoulder. Winston leisurely strolled up to the pole and pissed on the other dog's stain. Satisfied that his honor was restored, Winston rejoined Hoot at the front of the platoon.

Later that afternoon, we were again tested and evaluated. Our first stop was classification processing, where we were assigned the job "best suited to our preference, our ability and training, and the needs of the Marine Corps." This was a roundabout way of getting the paperwork done to clear our way into the infantry.

We took a battery of aptitude tests and those who could type, took a typing test to see if they could be "Remington Raiders."

We were then given a list with the names of all Marine Corps Military Occupational Specialties and told to mark our preferences. I marked radio announcer, newspaperman and public relations specialist.

I was then called into an office where a real officer, a captain, sat behind a desk. He glanced at my file and then looked up at me.

"I see you've been to six months of electronics school. Have you an interest in going to radio school?"

"No, sir," I boomed. I waited for him to tell me that I would then be going to radio announcer school.

"Congratulations, private," he leaned back in his chair, putting my file on a large stack, "you're in the infantry. Dismissed."

And don't let the door hit you in the ass on your way out. It was a short game; the score; "needs of the service": one, "my preference": zero.

We spent our evening learning how to "spit-shine" our dress shoes and shine our brass belt buckle with "Brasso." We also got to write another letter home. This one was to Wild Thing to let her know I had landed and the situation was in hand. I hated to lie like that, but I didn't want some sailor who had played softball through his 8-week Navy boot camp to take over, either.

After we did the high jump maneuver to get in our racks, Hoot proceeded to tell us about General Puller.

"Lieutenant General Lewis Burwell Puller is one of the most famous Marines who ever lived. He was awarded five Navy Crosses, an award second only to the Medal of Honor. Chesty Puller was always for the troops. One time a town near a Marine base was serving watered-down beer to the Marines on liberty. After a hard day of ground pounding, a Marine is entitled to real beer. That pissed Chesty off so bad that he started a Sherman tank company to run down and crack all the streets in the town. When Washington called to order him to recall the tanks, he decided to install beer machines in the barracks. Chesty has done everything you turds are being asked to do. So each night we will wish Chesty 'good night.' Let me hear it, girls, 'Good night, Chesty, wherever you are.'"

"Good night, Chesty," we screamed from our prone positions in our racks, "wherever you are!"

Chesty seemed like the first decent damn Marine so far.

Even though Hoot got in my face several times, I never felt the degree of fear I felt with the Frog, Sword, or especially, Snake. Impressed, yes, but I never believed he would do anything to me that my big brother hadn't done already.

CHAPTER 5 – WE NEED MORE STUFF

Good Mornin' World

After reveille the next morning, Sgt. Gibson told us to get ready to go to morning chow.

"Okay, clowns," he drawled, "when I give the word every swingin' dick will get outside and fall in. You will form three ranks according to height facing this building. Get outside!"

The swinging dicks and I swung on outside as we hurried to do his bidding. As we scurried to find our place in line, Sgt. Gibson strode out watching the pushing and running around.

"Knock off the grabassin' and get into line," he bellowed, hands on hips. "This isn't a hoedown where you swing your partner and skip to your goddammed Lou! In about two seconds, some of you are gonna get a little personal instruction!"

Immediately, our formation came to a standstill. He ambled to the rear of the platoon, looking at us shorter turds on the "Little End."

"How the hell did you little shits pass the height requirement? What the hell do you have to be? Five feet? You look like the goddamm Seven Dwarfs. And all of you turds are named 'Dopey' I'll bet."

"Arrrightt," he resumed, striding to the front of the herd, "we're going to sound off loud and clear 'good morning, world'! Let me hear it!"

"Good morning, world," we shouted.

"Bullshit, I can't hear you! Again!"

"Good morning, world," we screamed.

"Lemme hear your tigers roar!"

"Arrrggghhh," we growled.

"I didn't say 'meow' like a bunch of pussycats! You people are as useless as tits on a boar hog! I said let me hear you tigers *roar*!"

"Arrrrggghhh," we shrieked.

"Right, face!" We turned to the right. "Right, face!" he repeated.

We had turned around and were now facing away from the barracks.

"The commanding general lives across that field!" He pointed to a group of buildings about a half-mile away.

"I want the general to hear you pussycats *roar*!"

"Aarrrrrrrgghh," we roared for the general; even if he didn't come down to welcome us at the train station.

"Arright," he continued, "before we go to chow, you're going to learn 'dress right, dress.' You're going to extend your right arm and touch the shoulder of the turd on your right. If he's closer than the length of your arm, you're going to push him to the right. If he's further than that, you will grab his shoulder and pull him towards you. Got that?"

"When I say 'dress right' you wait until I say 'dress!' When I do, you will look over your right shoulder and put your hand out. Dress right," he hesitated, "Dress!"

The mob exploded to the right, accompanied by pushing and grabbing, turds stumbling, and those of us on the "little end" running to escape the rippling tide of bodies surging from the left. Finally, we became motionless and let our arms fall by our sides.

"Who in the hell told you could put your arms down," Hoot screamed, walking into the mob, jerking arms up. "Nobody told you to put your arms down! Get your arms up! Keep looking to your right! *I'll tell you* when to put your arms down!"

"Are you afraid to touch him, turd? Get over here!" Hoot jerked a turd by the arm, pulling his hand until it rested on the next turd's shoulder.

"Every hand should be on a shoulder! This is to get the proper distance between ranks so you can march without falling all over yourselves! This is thirty inches. You short armed people will have to extend your fingers. You orangutans will have to ball your fists. I want thirty inches!"

The "dress right, dress" maneuver performed outside our luxury accommodations. Photo courtesy of United States Marine Corps.

Hoot strode around the ranks; physically adjusting the short arms and orangutan arms until the desired thirty inches was met.

"Okay, that's about as close as you're going to get. I am now going to say 'ready, front.' When I say 'ready' you will not do anything. This is the preparatory command. It's a warning to you dumb shits that I'm going to give an order. When I say 'front', you will snap your head to the front and stop resting your hand on your neighbor's shoulder. You will drop your arms smartly to your side. You orangutans will try not to bounce your knuckles on the deck. Okay, listen up! Ready, front!"

Everyone did so, except one barrel-chested turd who was slow to lower his hand.

"You there, Buffalo Butt," Hoot screamed, "get your ass out here!"

My bunkmate, the turd designated "Buffalo Butt", shambled out of the herd and stood at attention in front of the drill instructor.

"You like taking your sweetass ole time, Buffalo Butt?" his spit spraying the turd's face. "You like your leisure, do you?"

"No, sir," yelled the Butt.

"Get down and give me twenty pushups! Maybe that will improve your hearing."

Buffalo Butt, who seemed to be all chest and shoulders with short bandy rooster legs, dropped to the ground and pushed up twenty times in short order. He jumped to his feet and stood at attention.

"Who told you to get up, turd? Get down for twenty more!"

The Butt whipped through another twenty and held himself expectantly off the ground.

"You find pushups easy, Buffalo Butt?"

"Yes, sir," the Butt shouted at the ground. Dumb shit.

"Ohhhh, you dooo? Its no wonder," Hoot observed,

putting his foot on the Butt's buttocks, "you got no goddammed *ass*! Gimme twenty more!"

Buffalo Butt strained, slowly pushing himself up against the strain of Hoot's foot.

"You still find them easy, turd?"

"No, sir," the Butt gasped.

"How many is that?"

"Seven, sir!"

"Bullshit," Hoot scoffed, "you're not doing them right. You gotta push your chest and ass *off* the ground. That's why they call them pushups. Start again!"

"One," the Butt wheezed. "Two, three, four..."

"Whoa, stop, hold it!"

Buffalo Butt stopped in mid push up, grateful for the break.

"I didn't hear 'sir,' Buffalo. What's the first word out of your mouth?"

"Sir, Sir," the miserable Buffalo Butt yelled.

"I can *hear*, you stupid shit. You don't have to repeat things to me! 'Sir, sir,'" he mocked. "Stop stuttering and sound off 'one, sir, two, sir'. Begin!"

"One, sir, two, sir" and Buffalo Butt was left to complete his count, unhindered except for Hoot's foot on his hind quarters.

"On your feet! You think you can put your arm down with everyone else?"

"Yes, sir," Buffalo Butt sounded confident that he could.

"Get back in the mob!"

Buffalo Butt soared into the relative safety of the herd.

"I can see that it's gonna take about a year and a half to graduate you people. You people got *shit* for brains!"

Ricochet to Forest Lawn

Sgts. Sword and Snake picked us up after noon chow and we moved on to more military activities, like picking up "782," or field gear, at the equipment shed. We were directed to file by wooden bins filled with such things as canteens, bayonets, cartridge belts and to take one of each. The items were definitely second-hand, some of which had probably seen service at the Battle of the Argonne in World War I. I shopped each bin for a newer, World War II item as time would permit. After a dozen or so trips, we had piles of what they called "782 gear."

To make sure every turd had the necessary marching and fighting gear, the supply sergeant picked up the first item and held it over his head.

"This is a canteen," he yelled. "everyone hold up his canteen!"

Everyone had a canteen.

"This is a cartridge belt! Everyone hold up his cartridge belt!"

"You, turd in the second rank," SSgt. Sword accused, "you got a cartridge belt?"

Sgt. Snake marched to the offending turd and grabbed his Adam's apple.

"Well, Four Eyes," he shouted at the bespectacled turd, "do you have a belt?"

Four Eyes just stood there, swallowing, his face ashen.

"Get your ass up there and get a cartridge belt!"

Four Eyes took off at a dead run, grabbing a belt from the supply sergeant and dropping it on his pile.

This is a cartridge belt. Did you get one?
Photo courtesy of United States Marine Corps.

"Okay," the supply sergeant continued, "everybody hold up his bayonet!"

"Jesus Christ, *no*," Sgt. Snake screamed at Four Eyes. "where in the hell's your bayonet?"

Four Eyes' lower lip quivered, his eyes filling.

"What the hell were you doing when the rest of these imbeciles were getting their bayonets? Playing hide and go seek? Did they *hide* the goddamned thing from you? Speak up!"

At this, Four Eyes' face crinkled and he started to cry.

"Jesus Christ," Snake moaned. "You goddammed baby! You pussy! Stop your sniffling and get your sorry ass up there and get a bayonet!"

Four Eyes made no move. He stood there crying even harder, sobbing like he was alone in the world. Which he was.

SSgt. Sword strode over to him and put his hand on the turd's shoulder.

"Come with me," Sword said almost gently. He steered Four Eyes over to the side of the herd. I was close enough to hear what was said.

"Where are you from, Four Eyes?"

"Forest Lawn, New York, sir."

"Don't you want to go back to Forest Lawn as a Marine?"

"No, sir," Four Eyes blubbered, "I just want to go home!"

"You don't want your girlfriend and your dad to think you couldn't make it here, do you?"

"I want to go *home*," Four Eyes persisted.

Sword stared at him, considering for a long minute, then turned to Snake.

"Call 'POU' and tell them we have one for them."

POU was the Psychiatric Observation Unit and going there meant you were "unregimented to military life." Another name for Funny Farm. The wind blew, and the shit flew. And there stood Private Four Eyes. But not for long, because in a couple of days, Four Eyes would be on his way to Forest Lawn. Hopefully, his parents hadn't already rented out his room. And we lost another.

I kind of felt sorry for Four Eyes as I had been close to tears a couple of times myself. But if truth be known, it wasn't a hard thing to walk past a bin and pick up a cartridge belt or a bayonet. All of the rest of us imbeciles were able to do it. Maybe his sorry ass was best out of here. I took some small measure of pride that I was a better man than he.

I wondered how many more Humpty Dumpties would fall. In less than three days, we had lost ten percent of the platoon. At this rate, in about thirty days Sgts. Sword, Snake, and Gibson would be marching each other to chow. And I was probably a Humpty Dumpty in the making.

We returned to the barracks minus Four Eyes, noting his laundry bag and towel were missing from his rack. It was like he was never there.

Holiday on Asphalt

SSgt. Sword had us fall out for our first visit to the parade ground, a half mile square of asphalt called the "grinder." We again lined up by height in three files. This was called Landing Party Manual, or LPM.

Reaching in and pulling out turds by height and stuffing them toward the front or rear of each line until they were satisfied, Sgts Sword and Snake arrived at a gently sloping herd. The tallest turds were well over six feet tall and the shortest a tad over five feet.

I ended up sixth shortest and again found myself in the next to last row.

"You will always line up in this position," Sword barked. "Look at the turd on either side, in front and in back of you. It would be better for you to remember your position than for me or Sgt. Snake to help you find it next time."

"When I say 'forward, march' you will step off with your left foot," Sword explained again. "I will tell you which foot to put down. I will say 'left' and your left foot will hit the deck. I will say 'right' and your right foot will hit the deck."

We had previously been over this. True, we had not done well.

"You will take a thirty-inch step. Not two feet, not a yard, but thirty inches. The 'Big End' will take a thirty-inch step or the 'Little End' will end up running to catch up. This," Sword took a step, "is a thirty inch step!"

"All right! I'm going to give the order 'forward, march' and you will step off on your left foot! We will left, right, left, right it for a while and then we might even try cadence. All right, here we go. Forward, harch!" It was obvious that there was a silent "m" in "march" but where did the "h" come from?

The herd lurched forward, up and over some turds that didn't get the word. Half a dozen feet were stepped on, causing a few turds to stumble.

"Whoa, mob! Whoa, herd! Stop," SSgt. Sword bellowed, "stand still, Goddammit! You people think you're on Bandstand? You think this is some kind of rock and roll dance?"

"What've you got: shit for brains and shit in your ears? How in the hell are you people going to march if you can't even take a single goddamned step! You just committed a 'FUBAB!' You people are 'Fucked Up Beyond All Belief!' When you have a FUBAB you get extra instruction! Get down for pushups! One!"

We dropped to our hands and toes on the asphalt and delivered twenty pushups per the requirements of FUBAB.

"On your feet! Line up! Get back into line! Hurry up!"

"Okay, kiddies," SSgt. Sword mocked, "we're going to do the Kindergarten Shuffle. When I say 'forward, march' you will take one step with your left foot and freeze in that position. Like this," Sgt Sword extended his left foot and froze. "This is what I want you to do."

We got the first step down pat and went on to the next task.

"Get your feet together! When I say 'forward, march,' this time you will keep walking. I will say 'left, right, left, right' and your left and right feet *will* hit the deck accordingly."

"Forwarrrd, Harch! Left, right, left, right! Your other left, Numb Nuts! Left," he paused, "left!"

Several turds had to skip occasionally to get on the step, but after half a mile or so, most were frequently on the correct foot. One turd kept falling on his face. At least he was making forward progress.

"Whoa, herd! We're going to learn to stop now. When I say the words 'platoon, halt' you will stop marching. The preparatory command is 'platoon' and you know I'm going to give the command 'halt.'"

Sword started marching. "I give the command 'platoon' you just keep marching, but you will wake up out of your trance and get ready to stop. Halt!"

Sword took one more step and stopped, putting his heels together. "I took one more step and brought my other foot beside the other and stopped. Like so", he took a couple of steps and halted again.

"Okay, we will try it. Forward, Harch! Left, right, left right! Whoa! Stop! Stop! You on the Little End!" He pointed to the turd on my left.

"Get out here!"

"How many feet do you have, turd?"

"Two, sir," the turd screamed.

"Then why are you taking three steps when I say 'left, right?' That's two counts but you're taking three steps. How in the hell are you doing that, turd?" Sgt. Sword stuck his nose in the turd's face.

"Sir, the private doesn't know!"

"You got a middle leg that you go pole vaulting on," Sword accused, "is your crank so long it's getting in the way?"

"No, sir!"

"Get down for pushups! We'll see if you can do a few without some abnormality that interferes with you putting down just two feet. Or maybe you'll go pole vaulting all over the parade ground. One!"

The unfortunate turd tried a push up.

"You got a hard on, turd?"

"No, sir!"

"Don't lie to me, turd! Give me twenty! Pound that sonofabitch in the asphalt! Get rid of it!"

The turd pounded off the remaining pushups without wobbling or pole vaulting and Sword let him rejoin the platoon. We committed a few more FUBABs and a new offense, called a "FUBAR." To "Fuck Up Beyond All Repair" costs forty pushups. After we "marched" for an hour or two, we took an off ramp and arrived at the armory.

He's Not Heavy

This was the moment I was waiting for; picking up my rifle at the armory! I had been preparing for this day for years; first with my cap gun, then my Red Ryder BB gun, and finally, a single-shot .22 rifle. I was a hell of a shot when we played cowboys and Indians, or war. But this was the real thing. This was a very *serious* thing.

As each turd filed by to receive his rifle, both the armorer and SSgt. Sword carefully inspected it, making note of any imperfections. The armorer wrote down the serial number and instructed us to memorize it. The rifle was heavier than I had expected, some nine and a half pounds.

Outside, the armorer gave us a brief lecture on the importance of this event.

"You are holding in your hands U.S. Rifle, Caliber .30, M1. The M1 Rifle is a gas-operated, clip-fed, air-cooled, semi-automatic shoulder weapon. It is the most *important* piece of equipment you will ever be issued! You must care for it like a *brother*! You will clean it, polish the stock and keep a fine layer of oil on it. Letting your rifle rust is a court martial offence!"

He held up a small notebook, which had been issued with each rifle.

"You will turn to page two in your scorebooks and read aloud with me!"

"This is my rifle," we yelled. "there are many like it, but this one is mine. My rifle is my best friend. It is my life. I must master it as I master my life."

This was indeed serious stuff. I felt like I had just given birth. We continued on to the other serious stuff.

"My rifle is human, even as I, because it is my life. We will become part of each other. Thus, I will learn it as a *brother*. I will learn its weaknesses, its strengths, its parts, its barrel, its sights, and its accessories. I will keep my rifle clean and ready, even as I am clean and ready. We will become part of each other. We will....before God I swear this creed."

I was sort of awed and hoped I would not let my rifle down. But at last, I was now in charge of *something*. It was a terrible responsibility, though, and I wondered if it could rust overnight when I wasn't looking.

CHAPTER 6 – DOWN TO BUSINESS

Command Performance

We returned to the parade ground with our U.S. Rifles, Caliber .30, M1. We were marching, and I use the term loosely, with our rifles bouncing on our right shoulders.

As we scuffled along, I could hear some part of my beloved rifle jingling. The further we marched, the louder the jiggling became. I knew that I was about to lose a part of my rifle, my brother, my life. My heart thudded and I couldn't stop swallowing.

"Get your heads up," SSgt. Sword yelled, "keep your eyes to the front!"

Tinkle, tinkle. Silence. *Ohhmigod!* Part of my rifle, part of my best friend, my *brother*, had fallen on his ass on the asphalt!

"Sir," I screamed.

"Shaddup on the Little End," bellowed SSgt. Sword.

I marched several more feet in misery, knowing I was damned. Either way I would die.

"Sir," I screamed again.

"Goddammit, I told you to shut up! Platoon, Halt! Whoa, herd! Stop! Who was yelling on the Little End?"

"Sir, Private..." I began.

"Get out here, turd! On the double! Now!"

"What the hell's your problem, Short Round?"

"Sir..." I began again.

"Speak up," SSgt. Sword demanded, grasping my

Adam's apple.

"Sir, part of the private's rifle fell off," I managed to rasp.

"Give me that," he slapped the rifle out of my grasp, spun it over, and inspected it.

"Not that it would probably do you any good, Deadeye, but you lost your rear sight aperture. You lost part of your weapon! Government property! The most important piece of equipment you will ever get!"

Without his rear peep sight, my brother was now blind, or at least needed glasses.

He shoved the rifle back into my hands, forcing me back a couple of steps.

"Get out there and find it! Go!"

I retraced our previous route on the double, my eyes glued to the ground. I heard SSgt. Sword and the platoon moving away. I redoubled my efforts, scurrying along the asphalt, occasionally sneaking glances to follow the location of my platoon. It passed and seemed to merge with other platoons, and in short order, I had no idea of which of the dozen or so marching platoons was mine.

After several minutes of scouring a half-mile square of black surface for a small piece of black metal, I began to understand more and more how a turkey must feel on the day before Thanksgiving.

I dropped to my elbows and knees, and canted my head to try to see if I could spot the inch-long aperture protruding above the flat surface. Nothing. I jumped to my feet to resume my frantic zigzagging.

Whupp! I collided with a solid, immovable chunk of humanity. The chunk shoved me back a few steps and stood glaring at me. He was a night club bouncer, dressed in green, wearing a Smokey Bear hat. He had no neck. On his sleeves he had three stripes up and four stripes down, with a star in the middle. Probably the Grand Kahuna of drill instructors everywhere.

"What in the hell are you doing, turd," he asked menacingly. "Are you *lost*?"

"Sir, the private lost his rear sight aperture and the drill instructor told the private to find it!"

"Which is your platoon, son," he asked almost humanely, glancing over the field at the marching platoons.

"Sir," I admitted miserably, "the private doesn't know."

He regarded me sadly. "You don't much like my Marine Corps, do you, son?"

"Yes, sir," I lied, "the private *does*!"

"You like my Marine Corps," he asked again, doubtfully.

"Yes, sir!"

"But do you *love* it, son? You've got to *love* my Marine Corps."

"Yes, sir!"

"Then let me hear it! 'I love the Marine Corps!' Sound off!"

"Sir, I love the Marine Corps!"

"Bullshit, you don't love my Corps. I can't hear you!"

"Sir, I love the Marine Corps!"

"Ohh, you're a goddammed inspiration," he said approvingly, "why, I think *all* the turds would want to hear that you love the Corps. See that reviewing stand over there?" He pointed across the field to wooden bleachers.

"Yes, sir!"

"Get over there and let me hear that you *love* the Corps."

"Aye, aye, sir," I yelled and set off for the stand. I raced up the tiers, faced the parade ground, and started affirming my love for the Corps.

"Sir, I love the Marine Corps!"

"Can't hear you," a voice boomed across the field.

"Sir, I love the Marine Corps!"

"Keep it up!"

"Sir, I love the Marine Corps!"

After a while, I noticed that the giant Smokey had snuck off to parts unknown. After several platoons of turds passed me by without so much as a glance, I began to feel abandoned. Actually, though, I was also beginning to enjoy a little independence.

As the platoons marched by, I imagined they were passing in review for my benefit. Good job, turds. Carry on.

Most platoons marched behind a turd carrying a pole with a red flag that identified the number of the platoon. Some platoons, like mine, had a turd marching up front with a pole, but no flag. The drill instructors were still too embarrassed to identify us, I supposed. I even spotted a small platoon of about twenty bliviks, puffing along under their flag, a red banner with a yellow elephant on it. The Fat Man's Platoon.

I began to vary my affirmations of love for the Marine Corps to entertain all the turds and bliviks in Turdville.

"Sir, I *love* the Marine Corps!"

"Sir, I love the *Marine* Corps!"

"Sir, I love the Marine *Corps*!"

Finally, after what seemed an hour or so, a green herd

stopped in front of the parade stand and SSgt. Sword strode to the stand.

"Get down here! What the hell are you doing up there?"

I related my collision with the drill instructor with the seven stripes and the ensuing conversation. Looking around, he asked if the seven-striper had asked what the platoon number was.

When I told him no, he told me to get the hell into ranks pronto and we hotfooted it out of there.

When we got back to the barracks, SSgt. Sword inspected our shoes and rifles. Just before taps, he addressed us as we were standing in front of our racks in skivvies and T-shirts.

"Reach down and grab your balls. They may not be much now but when you graduate, if you graduate, you will have a pair. Do you have any hair on your chest? Well, you will when you get out of here."

What about Buffalo Butt? He had more hair on his *back* than any ten of us had on our head. I resolved to grow an acceptable pair of balls and the treasured hair on my chest. I wondered if the saltpeter, which was rumored to be in our food, would retard the growth of my wedding tackle.

I Have Not Yet Begun To Exercise

After morning chow, SSgt. Sword marched us down a sandy road to a sandy field. Anything that wasn't sandy on Parris Island was either paved, or had a building on it. Charles Atlas, dressed in red shorts and a gold T-shirt with the red letters "USMC" on it, stood by on a raised wooden platform, possibly to kick some sand in our faces.

"I am your physical training, or 'PT,' instructor," Chuck announced. "Today we are going to learn how to do some exercises to strengthen your bodies."

"How many of you played high school football," the PT instructor asked. This sounded suspiciously like the setup SSgt. Sword used with the turd who was captain of the football team.

Nevertheless, about thirty hands shot up, their owners apparently expecting to try out for the Parris Island Football Team.

"Hey, that's *great*! You oughta be in good shape then. Get down for pushups." Bingo!

"How many of you turds played any high school sport? Basketball, baseball, tennis, intramural sports?" Another thirty reluctant hands went up.

"Good. Athletics are good. You oughta be in fairly good shape, too. Get down for pushups."

As a non-athlete, I was one of those who cheered as the winners ran by. I was too short for basketball and too light for football. I was generally the last one picked for a team. Where did that leave me?

"That leaves the rest of you. Get down for pushups. You people *need* to get into shape."

Why didn't he say "all of you get down for pushups" in the first place?

"Okay, from now on we do pushups the right way," Chuck advised, dropping to the pushup position. "On the count of 'one', we lower our bodies to the ground. Hold your body about an inch above the ground. On 'two' we push our bodies up with a snap. We hold our bodies in this position, keeping our body straight and rigid. We hold a long count, keeping our knees and stomach off the ground."

If God wanted recruits to put pushups on their resume', he would have attached their hands to their chests.

The instructor showed us how to do sit-ups, side

straddle hops, squat thrusts, squat jumps, pull-ups, along with every other strenuous exercise known to man. To his credit, he did all the exercises with us, dozens of them. He never seemed to have a hair out of place or broke a sweat.

But then what would you expect from someone who did pushups for a living?

The rest of us gutted through the whole arsenal of conditioning exercises, cursing his inhumanity and attempts to set new records for time and numbers of completions. He seemed to be convinced that we could exercise the enemy to death.

"Once we have completed sufficient exercises to obtain some upper body strength, we will have a field meet. All work and no play makes Turd a dull maggot."

Darrell Dottle

Other than pushups, sit-ups and such, drilling was our drill instructors' favorite pastime. Someone said that's why they were called *drill* instructors. Everyday there was always more than enough time for marching on the parade ground.

Two drill instructors would always go with us, one marching alongside calling cadence, and the other attacking any part of the ranks at will, screaming, shoving, and giving individualized training tips.

Today SSgt. Sword marched alongside in his usual position, giving us the left, right, left, right step. Sgt. Snake was in his favorite role, rushing up to this or that turd, threatening, stamping on feet, squeezing Adam's apples, and bending arms and backs.

"You people will keep marching as I call cadence," SSgt. Sword advised. "Listen for 'left' and 'right' as I call the cadence. One is left, two is right and three is left again."

"One, two, *three*, your *left*, two, *three*, your *left*!"

That sounded simple enough and kept most of us in step. Certainly this was more of an "official" marching routine than "left-righting" it everywhere. We were progressing down the road to being real Marines.

After a while, SSgt. Sword departed and we were again at the mercy of Sgt. Snake. He left-righted us for a while, then told us to listen up for cadence.

The trademark of the drill instructor is his cadence. No two DIs use the exact same cadence and some adopt a sing-song version. We listened intently to hear Snake's version.

"Darrell dottle duh darr, darrell dottle duh darr!"

What the hell was that? There was no "left" or "right" or "one" or "two" or "three" or anything recognizable in the whole damn thing. There was no melody, nor chorus. Give us a clue, I thought. A quartet of croaking bullfrogs had more rhythm than he did. If we marched as fast as he gargled they'd have to put speed bumps on the parade ground.

"Listen up, goddammit! Keep on the step!"

"Darrell dottle duh darr, darrell dottle duh darr!"

There it was again. What the hell language was he yodeling in? I strained to listen, but had no idea where "left" or "right" was. And he seemed proud enough, like he was saying mass or something profound.

I glanced down at my fellow turds' feet and tried to do what they did.

"You people on the Little End better get in step!"

No help there. I looked forward to the Big End and hoped they understood enough of the throat-clearing harangue to set the example.

"Do you people understand English," he screamed. "Get on the step!"

"Darrell dottle duh darr, darrell dottle duh darr!"

After getting out of step several times, I realized that I knew less about how to walk than I used to. I knew I would never get out of boot camp unless I got a "Darrell Dottle" dictionary. I trudged along, expecting Snake to jump in front of my face at any moment and ask me if I had shit for brains.

Wait a minute! Snake had to be on the step or he couldn't tell if we weren't! I sneaked looks out of the sides of my eyes and tried to match Snake's strides.

"Keep your eyes to the front! This isn't a goddammed sight-seeing trip!"

We "marched" along a few paces to the gargling accompaniment of Sgt Snake. Half of the turds were constantly off the step he had in mind.

"Whoa, mob," he screamed. "you maggots have just committed a FUBAR! Not only are you Fucked Up Beyond All Belief, you are "Fucked Up Beyond All Repair!" If you people on the Little End don't get with the program we're going to be out here till taps. Get down for pushups! *One*!"

Sonofabitch had eyes in the back of his head. I had to find somebody who understood "darrell dottle," and fast.

CHAPTER 7 – CLEAN UP YOUR ROOM

Field Day

With our testing and equipment issue completed, we were looking forward to "field day," which was supposed to occur the next morning. In the recruiting brochures we had seen pictures of recruits playing football and other track events, sitting around talking, and even laughing. We were ready for a break.

SSgt. Sword gave us the bad news after morning chow.

"You people will 'field day' this squadbay and head. First and Second squads will wash the windows and the Third and Fourth squad will clean the head. The Fifth and Sixth squads will sweep, scrub and buff the deck."

"You will strip your racks and stack your sheets, pillow case, and fartsack on the deck in front of your rack. You will turn over your mattress! You will then fold your blanket and place it with your pillow on the mattress. Each squad leader will assign one man to collect all the linen from his squad in a fartsack and place it outside my hatch! Get hot!"

What the hell was a "fartsack?" I stripped off my blanket, two sheets and pillowcase. The only things that were left were the mattress and the mattress cover. It must be the mattress cover! I saw the rest of the turds taking the cover off the mattress and stacking it with the sheets. It was bad enough that the mattress was only two inches thick; did the damn thing *fart,* too?

The floors, or decks, were of plain wood. No curtains or Venetian blinds adorned the many windows, allowing us to know when the sun came up. It probably also helped the Corps save money on electricity.

Furniture consisted of two rows of bunks, complete with 2-inch mattresses, two rifle racks and a 50-gallon galvanized garbage can. No couches, no pinball machines.

Our bunks were called racks. Probably a holdover from the days when they used to stretch turds on them. Snake had missed his time but probably had a pillory stashed behind the barracks somewhere.

Our only luxury item was our locker box, a wooden crate with a lid and removable shelf which held our clothes, toilet supplies, and writing paper. We used it as a chair when we cleaned our rifle, shined our shoes, wrote letters or attended classes in the squad bay. No foot rest. We weren't permitted to sit on our racks, or God forbid, lay on them before taps.

The turds of the Fifth and Sixth squads and I swept the deck, got down on our hands and knees with our buckets and scrub brushes and scoured the floor. We dried the deck with old blankets and laid down a layer of milky wax. Then we buffed the wax with an antique electric buffer that looked like an upside down ceiling fan from a Belgian Congo way station.

Because the "buffer" was not heavy enough to put a decent shine on the wooden surface, I, being one of the smallest turds, was elected to sit on it while a larger turd operated the buffer. It was a wild ride as my steed and I frequently crashed into racks, locker boxes, and several times, the bulkhead. The electric buffer smelled like it was burning up and I worried that I would be electrocuted at any moment. Being behind schedule, my fellow squad members also had to drag some of the other smaller turds around the floor on blankets to help "buff" the floor.

The window cleaners had no better equipment. They used water and vinegar to clean the glass windowpanes. Folded brown paper towels completed their cleaning gear.

The head detail had it the worst, however. Not only did they have to scour the tile floor and clean the mirrors; they also had to clean the urinals, sinks, and eight porcelain "thrones." That meant shining all the fixtures and faucets as well. Needless to say, no one was allowed to use the facilities during field day.

Sword checked on our progress, rejecting several windows, murky patches of wax on the deck, and cruddy urinals and sinks.

"Get those spots on the deck buffed! There are still streaks on the windows! I will return for inspection in thirty minutes! If the squadbay passes, we will go to chow. If it doesn't, we will scrub the deck again and start over!"

Everybody turned to with new vigor and I had a few more death defying rides on the whirling dervish. Finally, it was as good as the inside of a converted World War II chicken coop could look.

Sword appeared at the appointed time and we held our breath as he looked in every nook and cranny. Without even so much as a "thank you, good job, turds," he told us to get outside for chow.

"Field day" was a misnomer. We saw nothing that even remotely resembled a field. The good news was that it didn't take all day.

Mowing the Grass

Next to my rifle, my brother and best friend, the next most important piece of equipment issued to me was my bucket. Only a two-gallon galvanized wash bucket, to be sure, but it was an integral part of my everyday life.

We used our buckets when washing our clothes, cutting the grass, policing the area, and for smoking. During smoking, this versatile piece of equipment was used as a stool or as a helmet.

"Get outside with buckets and bayonets!"

We lined up in formation, buckets in one hand and bayonets in the other.

"You turds in the front rank will police the area. You will walk shoulder to shoulder down to the corner, turn left and go around the back of the barracks and return to this spot. You will pick up any garbage, dirt, dog turds and sea gull shit on the street and on the area around the barracks. You will pick up everything not nailed down or growing! Get hot!"

Police the area and pick up everything not nailed down or growing. Did that mean you had to inform a piece of garbage "you're under arrest" before you picked it up?

"You turds in the second rank will cut the grass on the front and on the left side of the barracks. The third rank will cut the grass in the rear and on the right side of the barracks. You will reach down, grab the grass and cut it with your bayonet. You will cut to a uniform height of three inches! Move out!"

Our barracks were two-story World War II H-shaped buildings supported on concrete blocks about three or four feet above the sand. This was apparently to keep flood tides, snakes, and alligators from cruising on into our squad bays and showing up for reveille. The buildings were white shingled affairs with metal fire escapes on the ends. Two platoons of 75 men lived on the ground floor and topside of each leg of the "H" while the drill instructors lived in "huts" on the passageway connecting the legs of the "H."

In the rear of each building were the flat concrete wash racks where we washed our clothes. Behind the racks were the drill instructors' parking lots and large live oaks, Spanish Moss hanging from their limbs.

Steam pipes on elevated poles graced the street and

completed the architectural design for the area. It was known as "Dodge City," which probably gave Snake his fantasy about drawing on us.

The first rank picked up everything from twigs, pebbles and even dust and placed it in their buckets. Several turds crawled on their hands and knees, whetting their fingers and dipping them into the dust to accomplish their mission.

Being in the second rank, I was entrusted to cut the grass to a uniform level. I scalped the grass with gusto, pretending that I was separating Sgt. Snake's sparse hair from his scalp. I permitted myself a mild case of rejoicing as I brought in the sheaves.

We had been told that it cost the U.S. taxpayers seventeen times as much to support one "Wing Wiper" in the U.S. Air Force as it did for one Marine. I'd say they saved at least three times as much just on lawn mowers alone. When you threw in gasoline and oil, it all added up.

A problem arose when Rank One happenchanced on a few turds deposited on the lawn by the canine Cpl. Winston. No one wanted to pick up the turds, or worse yet, get their bucket dirty with a turd.

Sgt. Snake, seeing the hesitation of three turds on the policing detail, strode over and inspected the ground.

"These turds aren't fertilizer! They're not nailed down or growing! Pick them up!"

"Aye, aye, sir," they yelled.

The nearest turd reached over, sizing up the turd.

"It's not a goddammed *grenade*, turd! It won't *explode*! Pick it *up*!"

Turd No. One gingerly picked up a turd and dropped it in his bucket. The turd had aged a little, and clunked as it hit the bottom of the bucket. He started to pick up another turd while the other two recruits stood by.

"No, no," Snake coached, "don't hog all the turds. There's enough for us all!"

"You, turd," he grabbed the shoulder of Turd No. Two and propelled him forward. "get down there and get your turd!"

Turd No. Three needed no prompting and snapped up the remaining turd and dropped it into his bucket.

"See there, turds, that's what we call teamwork!"

Snake went into the barracks and left us to our grass scalping and turd removal. We manicured the designated area, gleefully and secretly burying another of Cpl. Winston's deposits in Snake's absence.

All too soon, Snake reappeared, inspecting the area. Keeping his eyes on us turds, he tripped on a clump of grass, almost falling.

That was wonderful, Super Turd, I silently chuckled to myself. Do they have any more like you at home? I guess it's too much to hope for that you get hit with a meteor or a falling piece of Kryptonite.

"There are too many high spots in the lawn," he pronounced. "Rank Two will go around again, leveling out the high spots."

Duz does Everything

"Ranks One and Three will take their laundry bags, soap, scrub brushes and buckets to the wash racks. You will wash the dog shit out of your buckets before you wash your clothes. Some of you probably are used to living in crap and would wear the same clothes for a month if we let you."

"Your skivvies and utilities are filthy, dirty, skuzzy! We promised your Mommy you'd be wearing clean skivvies in case you get hit by a tank or a six-by truck and have to go to the dispensary."

The wash racks were cement tables where we had the opportunity to revert back to the pioneer method of washing clothes.

We laid out our clothes as flat as we could, considering we had very little space with all the other turds trying to get the same job done at once. We filled our buckets with water and soaked our clothes, poured in some Tide, then laid out the clothes and scrubbed with our brushes. Because of many pushups on the grass and dirt, we had to work hard to brush the stains out. We then wrung our clothes out and fastened them to the clothes line with "tie ties," thin little pieces of rope of no account. I guess the pioneers didn't have clothespins either.

After a day on the clothesline, the utilities were relatively dry. Dry or not, they came down, sometimes to get their final drying from body heat. Damp clothes weren't so bad; it was the soap streaks that really stood out.

Rubadubdub. Photo courtesy of United States Marine Corps.

After laundry time, Hoot treated us to a smoke. The "smoking lamp" was lit about two times a day; sometimes not at all.

A Dirty, Disgusting Habit

Those of us that didn't smoke when we arrived soon started to smoke. Since we were assumed to be in better physical shape than smokers, the drill instructors had us stay in the barracks and do pushups while the smokers smoked.

"Smokers, with one cigarette and your bucket, get outside!"

After falling out in two ranks, Hoot went through the drill. "With one match and a cigarette, light up!" If the match went out before you lit your cigarette, you pantomimed smoking because you didn't get a second chance.

"Arright, put your bucket on your head! One! Take a drag! Hold it! Two! Exhale!"

"Johnson! Do I see smoke coming out of your bucket? Hold those fumes in there! You paid for that cigarette and you're going to enjoy it!"

"Yes, sir," a muffled voice yelled.

"One! Two! One! Two!"

After four or five puffs, my eyes burned with the cloud of smoke building under my bucket. The title of the song "Smoke Gets in Your Eyes" forever took on new meaning for me.

"In battle, there will be smoke! 'One! Two!' That smoke will hurt your eyes. But you better keep your eyes open, because sometimes bad guys come through smoke trying to kill you. 'One! Two!'"

Was that cigar smoke I smelled? With my oversized

helmet, I couldn't see Hoot, but I knew he was smoking a cigar. Selfish bastard.

"Smoking is a dirty, disgusting habit.," the hypocrite lectured, "it causes forest fires and pollutes your lungs. It cuts down on how far you can run or how many pushups you can do. 'One! Two!' You people oughta think about quitting."

Since smoking was the only vice remotely possible in this asylum, I wasn't about to give it up.

"Okay, one verse of the Marine's Hymn. But since you are turds, not *Marines*, the last line is '*we'll be proud* to claim the title of United States Marine'. One! Two!"

We ran through a speedy version of the Hymn and were at last ordered to remove the buckets from our heads.

"Okay turds, take your buckets off your heads and put them on the deck."

A nearby forest ranger was probably shifting his binoculars to track the rising smoke cloud just released by the platoon.

"Sit on your bucket. That's right, Dumbass, sit *in* it! Don't ever have kids, Gooney Bird!"

As soon as I could see, I checked to see if Hoot had a cigar. He seemed innocent enough, but I knew he was guilty.

Hoot also showed us how to "field strip" our Pall Malls and Luckies when finished smoking. This entailed pulling a thin strip of paper down the side of the carcass so that the remaining tobacco could be rolled between our fingers and dispersed on the ground. We rolled up the paper into a tiny little ball and ate it. It tasted as good as one of the mess sergeant's peas.

Yes, it was only a bucket, but it was mine.

A little Serutan, Please

During the first several days, going to the bathroom was a problem. The bathroom, or head, consisted of three open areas: the shower room, the sink room, and the commode, or "throne room." The throne room boasted a line of open commodes on one side and a line of urinals on the other. Sitting on a commode with no partitions or doors was new to me and embarrassing to use. Moving my bowels was a very personal thing that I could only do at home. Some guys could sit and talk up a storm with their neighbors while relieving themselves and not miss a heartbeat. I practically got constipation before deciding to visit the throne room after taps, when everyone was in the sack.

There wasn't enough sinks for the shavers and I was usually shoved to the back of the line and had to wait until the bigger turds were done. My strategy to save time by lathering up and brushing my teeth while waiting in line, generally resulted in a Barbasol and Ipana cocktail.

Sometimes we ran out of time, so I just toweled off the lather and spit out the toothpaste. This happened often enough that the lather built up on the towel, making it a little stiff but serviceable. When I toweled off after a shower I'd get some lather streaks on my arms and legs. But when our towels were draped over the edge of our racks, mine always assumed a nicely creased look with the help of the excess lather.

CHAPTER 8 – A LITTLE EDUCATION IS A GOOD THING

The World, According to Hoot

One of the drill instructors lectured every evening on military history, sanitation, U.S. Rifle, Caliber .30, M1, military courtesy, rank structure, and a myriad of other topics.

One of our first lectures was given by Sgt. Gibson. He sat on a locker box in the center of the squadbay, surrounded by his kingdom of turds sitting on the floor with notebooks.

"The first topic is on hygiene. That means cleanliness and avoiding getting the clap."

"You will all take showers *everyday*! That means you soap down your entire body, including your ass and crotch. You will brush your teeth and shave everyday! Whether you need to or not. You will change your skivvies and socks everyday! You will wash your hands *every* time you make a head call! Even if you do not piss on your hands."

"How many of you have heard the lecture on the birds and the bees? Dirty-minded little animals," he observed without waiting for an answer. "How many of you know what a condom is? A rubber?" Again he continued without an answer.

"This is a rubber," he instructed, holding up a tin foil packet. Ripping the packet open, he displayed a circular web of rubber. He then produced a cucumber and stretched the rubber over it.

"Not that any of you are hung like this; you'll

probably have to put a tourniquet on the end of your dick to keep it from falling off. They don't make junior-sized rubbers for you pencil dicks."

"Later on, when you get liberty, if you ever get that far, you are not to run to the first whorehouse you can find. Most of you will be like the horny monkeys with the red asses you see at the zoo. Lying in the sack with Rosie Rottencrotch will give you the clap!"

"If you get a case of the Galloping Crud, you will pray you can learn to piss out of your foot. It is a painful disease that you can pass on to your girlfriend. You are also defacing government property, making you lose time by going to sick call for short arm inspection, instead of performing your duty. Always use a rubber."

"There are other things worse than the clap. Some guys in the Pacific picked up some really bad shit from the Rosie Rottencrotches in Okinawa and Korea."

"They had to haul their balls around in a wheelbarrow. A few went crazy with syphilis. Some other guys were afraid to come home, especially the married ones, because their wedding tackle just plain *fell off*!"

"I know some of you studs will still make a beeline for the first cathouse you see, but remember this! Every fifteen minutes, a member of the Marine Corps is setting himself up to catch a case of the clap!"

We have to *find* that horny sonofabitch, I thought self righteously, and stop him before he spreads an epidemic.

"Just keep this in mind: Don't crap in your mess kit!"

As profound a statement as I have ever heard, but what the hell did it have to do with venereal disease?

Sounds of running and mysterious thumping ensued from the turds living topside.

"Pay attention," Hoot growled, looking at the ceiling,

"we can always do what they're doing instead."

"Okay, enough about hygiene! The next topic is Marine Corps Rank Structure. Turn to page 40 in your Guidebook for Marines! There you see the rank and insignia for both enlisted ranks and officers."

"The rank of Private is the lowest rank there is. That's what you turds are. Everybody outranks you. You are lower than whaleshit, and you know where that is. Next, you have Private First Class, Lance Corporal, then Corporal. If you should ever make Corporal E-4, you will be senior to half of the entire Marine Corps."

Wow, if I ever make Corporal I'll have almost a hundred thousand troops at my command!

"Then we come to Sergeant, the most *important* rank in the Corps! It's the sergeants that get everything done!"

"We go to Staff Sergeant, Gunnery Sergeant, Master Sergeant, First Sergeant and Sergeant Major. The officers go from Warrant Officer up to General. There are eighteen ranks above you, so everybody will tell you what to do. If anybody tells you to do something, you do it, because there isn't any rank below whaleshit."

On the other hand, I was only eighteen ranks from taking over the Marine Corps. I could only move up; there wasn't any "down."

"You will be expected to know every rank in the Marine Corps as well as the Navy, Army, Air Force and Coast Guard! Now we're going to move on to Marine Corps History and Tradition! Listen up!"

"The Marine Corps was founded in a beer hall in Philadelphia on November *10th*, 1775. The beer hall was called Little Tun Tavern and was one of the most likely places to find recruits."

"The Navy was founded on November *18th*, 1775, eight days later. The Marine Corps needed a transportation arm and also somebody to provide some medical, dental and religious support. All the other services followed after that, with the Air Force, or 'Wing Wipers', being last."

"That's why the Marine Corps is called the Senior Service and why our color guards lead all parades. The Marine Corps is older than the country itself."

"The Marine Corps has a long and illustrious history. Many fine Marines who sat where you are sitting right now have died earning the title 'United States Marine.' That's why you people are turds. You haven't earned shit. You aren't even pimples on a Marine's ass. Someday you might be, but you have an awful lot to live up to."

"The Marine Corps builds men. This is where that happens, and we will do just that. If we have to kick your ass up over your shoulder, march you into the ground, teach you to shoot like Annie Oakley, and grow you a set of balls, we will."

"Someday you may be sitting in a foxhole and a thousand bad guys come charging up a hill, shooting at you. Do you want the guy sitting next to you tonight to be in that foxhole with you, protecting your back? Would he want *you* in there with him?"

"Some of you won't be there anyway, because you're not going to make it out of boot camp. Those of you that do will be proud and glad your buddy is in that foxhole with you. Because you know he's tough enough to stand his ground and shoot back. Marines have been doing that since 1775 and they will keep doing that as long as there's a Marine Corps."

I hoped with all my heart and soul that I could measure up.

"Okay, who can tell me who was awarded the first Mameluke Sword? When it was…" Hoot stopped, surprised, as Weezil actually raised his hand. *Nobody* ever raised their hand.

"Well," Hoot waited, nodding his head from side to side.

Weezil, smiling coyly, said, "Sir, was it Lt. Presley O'Bannon at the Battle of Tripoli?"

"Was it Presley O'Bannon? Is a pig's ass *pork*," Hoot demanded. "Does a bear shit in the woods? Does a cat have an ass? Of course it was Presley O'Bannon! *I'm* asking the fuckin' questions. You're providing the fuckin' answers!"

That'll teach you, Suckup, I thought.

"In your next free time, you are to read and study the sections in the Guidebook for Marines on History and Rank Structure. You will be asked questions on these subjects on the 60 day examination."

I couldn't believe the sonofabitch gave us homework.

"Arright," Gibson concluded, looking at his watch, "you people have ten minutes to make headcalls and get ready to hit the rack! When I come back in here, you will be standing in front of your rack in T-shirts and skivvies!"

When Gibson returned, he ordered us into our racks. Even the entry into our racks was a precise military maneuver, a crisp sideways jump, landing at the horizontal position of attention. The rack frames shook and screamed as the turds on the top rack high jumped into their rack.

"You will wish General Puller good night now."

"Goodnight, Chesty," we screamed, "wherever you are!"

Gibson turned out the lights and we climbed under the sheet and blanket in a military manner.

Getting Religion

On our first Sunday morning at Parris Island, we

were given the treat of sleeping in until 0600. After several 17-hour days, we had slept like the dead. After chow, Sgt. Gibson lined us up on the street outside the barracks.

"The Marine Corps wants you turds to have spiritual guidance," Hoot advised. "Therefore, this morning you are going to church. The Corps has churches for Bead Rattlers, Holy Rollers, and Kikes."

"You, turd," he pointed to his nearest turd, "what's your religion?"

"Methodist, Sir!"

"Get over to that fire hydrant. All Holy Rollers will form ranks on him! Go!" About half the platoon formed on the Methodist.

"What're you," he motioned to one of the remaining turds.

"Roman Catholic, sir!"

"Move off to that yellow line on the street! All Bead Rattlers will form ranks on him!" Another large group formed on the Bead Rattler.

"And you?"

"Sir, I'm a Latter Day Saint!"

"Get over there with the Holy Rollers!"

"You?"

"Greek Orthodox, sir!"

"Get over there with the Bead Rattlers!"

"Do we have any Kikes here?"

Three hands went up.

"You Kikes will form a line on Moses here!"

"What the hell are *you* people," he motioned to the four remaining turds.

"Sir, I'm an atheist," shouted the nearest turd.

"Not today, turd. I don't give a damn if you're Mahatma Fuckin' Gandhi! The Corps has three churches. You're either a Holy Roller, a Bead Rattler or a Kike. Pick one and get in line! All atheists pick a church!"

"And you, Mr. Moto," he asked a turd of Asian extraction.

"Sir, I am a Shinto!"

"What the hell is a Shinto," Hoot sounded baffled. "Sounds like some kind of Bead Rattler to me. Get over there with the Bead Rattlers! If that isn't right, next time go with the Kikes! Git!"

"Arright," Hoot lectured, pacing between the three groups, "you people may be fooled by the mild mannered chaplain at your church. He may be wearing a Marine uniform, but he is not a Marine. He is in the Navy and may take pity on your sorry asses! He will probably talk to you like you're civilians!"

"But remember this, you may lounge around church for awhile and while God may have your soul, your *ass* belongs to me!"

It was the first time I had ever been to a church that didn't have a collection. Not that I had any money to put in it. The Navy Chaplain was a concerned, understanding man.

"I know these days are hard for you," he consoled us, "leaving your homes and loved ones is hard. Your training program, I know, is challenging. Ask for His love and protection to bring you through. Pray to Him for the strength and the courage to carry out His Plan for you."

The Chaplain spoke calmly and reassuringly, lulling us into a semi-sleep. This was the first person that treated us like human beings since we got here.

I wanted church to last; especially since the Women

Marine boots were in attendance. They sat on the opposite side of the church with no chance of contact. No talking, no church social, no smiling. I did sneak a couple of looks their way, however, being the bold turd that I was.

I thought that I might turn out with the Bead Rattlers the next Sunday to get a look at their Women Marine boots.

Soon, all too soon, church was over and we reluctantly filed outside. There Sgt. Gibson stood waiting, hands on hips.

"Arright, Arright! Religion is over," Hoot announced to the faithful, "get your sorry asses in line!"

Marching With the Junior Birdmen

Later that afternoon, Snake took us to the "grinder" to rehearse our marching. We were his last platoon and Snake was determined that our platoon would be the Recruit Depot Drill Champions. He marched us unmercifully on the hot pavement for hours on end. He didn't believe in recess or time out so our tired feet just plodded along. These were the times that tried men's soles.

One of the DIs in our sister platoon had a cadence I could understand. It was a sad, sing-song cadence. "One, three, dot al lowll, fort ah lowll." I got so enthralled with his song I got out of step every time Snake and he were on the same parade deck.

Not that we could understand "Darrell Dottle" anyway, but Snake stopped calling his "cadence" as we marched past an oncoming platoon

Snake's idea was that we could "clomp, clomp" loud enough to keep in step while passing close by another platoon which was also going "clomp, clomp."

Unfortunate, our rival's platoon's "clomp, clomp" and Snake's substandard cadence caused several of our turds to falter, and soon half the platoon was on the wrong foot. Sgt. Snake, clearly embarrassed, let the other platoon gain some distance before he spoke.

"Whoa, mob, whoa herd! This is not a Ukrainian folk dance! Stop, goddammit! What the hell was *that*? That was like a shit sandwich! Unfuckingbeleivable! You people can't even walk, let alone march! You'll never be Marines! You shitheads wouldn't even make a pimple on a Marine's ass!"

Now that was *overkill,* I thought. By now, we could at least be a *pimple* on a Marine's ass.

Snake's ranting probably qualified for what Miss Biddy, my English teacher, called a "diatribe." A diatribe, she said, "was a prolonged discourse of abusive speech and satirical criticism." Therefore, a diatribe was an ass chewing. I felt a little better, having been subjected to something of a high minded nature and being able to use one of Miss Bitty's obscure vocabulary words, probably for the first of many times. I smiled to myself as I imagined Snake making poor Miss Bitty get down for pushups.

"Those letters on your shirts don't mean United States Marine Corps! No, for you turds, USMC means "Uncle Sam's Mouse Club!" This isn't a platoon; it's a *cartoon*!"

I tried to look properly chagrinned at this insult of insults, as did we all. I would have though "Uncle Sam's Masochistic Children" came in a close second.

"You're not Marines; you're the fucking Junior Birdmen!"

Again, I was not tremendously hurt by this outburst. Junior Birdman had it all over our present title of turd.

Snake gunned us down with his stare as he walked through the ranks. We wilted, melted, and shrank like groundhogs in their holes.

"Turn your covers around! They're not covers; they're party hats! Take them off and turn the bill backwards like you do at home!"

"Now turn your weapons around and lay them on your shoulders!"

We grasped our rifles by the muzzles and laid the stocks over our shoulders. I hoped my brother did not mind my holding him by his nose.

"That looks more like it! You *look* like a bunch of clowns. Okay, kiddies, we're going to skip along home! Move out! I said *skip*!"

"We're the Junior Birdmen," he chanted.

"We're the Junior Birdmen," we sang out, skipping along.

"Flying upside down!"

"Flying upside down," we chorused.

"We're the Junior Birdmen!"

"We're the Junior Birdman!" We were getting the skip now. It was a lot easier than "Darrell Dottle."

"With our noses to the ground!"

"With our noses to the ground!"

I thought it was nicely done, but Snake looked like he was choking.

"You people are a disgrace," he gritted, "some of you don't even know enough to be embarrassed! You don't know what pride is! You turds are an embarrassment to the Marine Corps!"

I'm afraid I was one of those that didn't know enough to be embarrassed. In fact, I thought it was kind of fun, one of our lighter hearted moments. After all, I had learned a new song and was definitely one of the best skippers.

True, it wasn't as funny as when the "WM's," or Women Marines, screwed up and sang "Yes, we have no bananas," but it wasn't bad. To break their little hearts even further, the WMs were told by their DIs that there was five miles of dick on the Island, and they were not going to get an inch of it. Not that we pencil dicks would know what to do with it anyway. It was true, at our age the biological clock made us oversexed but unsophisticated as a way of life.

Someday I would probably look back on all this and laugh. Trouble was, "someday" might come very soon, and I might be laughing *all day long* in some Navy funny farm.

CHAPTER 9 – SNAKE STRIKES AGAIN, AND AGAIN

Things That Go Bump

When we got back to the barracks, however, we soon discovered Sgt. Snake was a lot more disappointed than he first showed. He was still obviously very pissed when we placed our weapons in the rifle racks and stood in front of our bunks.

"Get down for pushups," he ordered. How pushups were going to help us march I couldn't fathom, but the imaginative Snake had his ways.

"When I call cadence, you will lean forward and bump your blockheads on the deck. If we can't pound sense into you pea brains on the drill field, we'll go directly to the source."

"Darrell dottle darl duh, darrell dottle darl duh," Snake gargled away.

We leaned forward and gingerly bumped our foreheads on the wooden floor.

"I don't hear anything," he screamed. "lean into it!"

The clunk of seventy-five foreheads on the deck continued for a few minutes while Snake drawled his unintelligible gibberish.

I wasn't anxious to pound what little brains I had out on the floor, so I took it easier than most. I thought I had it down pretty well, tapping my forehead on the floor, then drawing it up smartly, like it bounced off the floor.

"Okay! On your feet! What little intelligence you probably didn't have anyway is now gone, so now we can start all over!"

He grabbed the nearest recipient of the improvised frontal lobotomy and inspected his forehead. A lump had formed on the recruit's forehead. Snake marched the new dimwit to the head and turned the shower on his face.

"Form a line here! When I pass you through, you will move in the head, put your face under the shower, return to your rack and towel off! Move!"

Snake carefully inspected each bump.

Too late now, you sadistic bastard, I thought. If you find a bigger bump than you like, what are you going to do? Put a cast on the poor turd's head?

"Whoa, Sweetie," Snake accused, pulling a recruit out of line, "you don't like to beat your brains out on the deck?" He grabbed the offender's head and bonked it into an 8x8 wooden support beam. A satisfactory bump appeared immediately.

Judas Priest! Snake was not feeling sorry for the bumps! He knew precisely the minimum trauma he was looking for!

I, unfortunately, along with half a dozen others, would probably not pass bump inspection, and was destined to suffer a brief, but nodding acquaintanceship, with the beam. I suffered a hundred worse deaths as my turn approached.

I didn't pass, but mercifully it was over in a bonk, and I didn't even get a headache.

There was a fine line between insanity and sadism. Snake definitely fell on one side or the other, not that it mattered much which one.

I didn't learn a damn thing from the episode, except to watch the feet of my fellow turds out of the corner of my eye when Snake called what he claimed was "cadence." I wondered if I ever *would* understand it, and if I'd be normal, if I did.

Life Is Just a Box of Cherries

About a week or so after sending our "Dear mommy, we are having a wonderful time" letters, we had our first mail call.

"It looks like mommy has decided," announced an irritated Sgt. Snake, "probably against her better judgment, to own up and admit she has a turd in America's finest training camp!"

"When I call your name, you will double time around the squadbay, making all the corners, and as you approach, I will hold out your letter. You will jump in the air, clapping your hand on the letter, and keep going to your rack!"

"You will touch *only* the letter. You will *not* touch me! Do you understand?"

"Yes, sir!"

"When you get back to your rack you will slit the envelope open with your bayonet and spread the contents on the deck. Is that clear?"

"Yes, Sir!"

"Ajax!"

"Here, sir," Ajax shouted.

"I *know* you're here, you dumb shit. Where the hell else *would* you be? Out nightclubbin'? Get your ass up here!"

Ajax approached, leaped in the air and clapped his hands on empty air. Snake had withdrawn the letter at the last instant.

"You almost *struck me*, turd," he screamed, "did you mean to *strike* a non-commissioned officer in the performance of his duty?"

"No, sir," the shaken Ajax reassured the drill instructor.

"You had better not, Ajax! It would be the *biggest* mistake you ever made! Go around again!"

"Applegate!"

Turd Applegate zoomed around the squadbay, leapt into the air, and clapped the letter cleanly, without touching Snake. Ajax followed close on his heels, but Snake did not extend the letter.

"Keep going, Ajax," Snake sneered, watching Ajax again clap at empty air.

The rest of mail call went relatively civil until all the letters were handed out. After completing a few dozen laps, Ajax wheezed up to get the last one.

Snake toured the rectangle of the squadbay, flipping over the letters, newspaper clippings, and pictures with his swagger stick. He balled up and tossed several clippings in which turds were considered heroes for joining the Corps, and pronounced that the girls who had sent pictures had poor taste in men. No cyanide pills were discovered.

"Now, we have a special letter," Snake announced, holding up a small box wrapped in brown paper. "Where is Private Weezil?"

"Here, Sir!" It was the turd who wouldn't let me plug my electric shaver in on the first morning and who liked to judge pushups.

"Get your ass up here!"

Weezil made a point of running hard, like he was trying out for the Olympics, and stood groveling at Snake's feet.

"Unwrap it!"

Weezil's hands shook as he unwrapped the box.

"What have we here," Snake asked pleasantly, tapping the box with his swagger stick, "chocolate covered *cherries*! My favorite! Who was it that sent you this wonderful present, Sweetie?"

"The private's Aunt Sally, Sir!"

"Well come along, Sweetie," Snake chortled, "we'll want to make sure you'll remember to thank Aunt Sally for sending you such a treat. Especially when you were instructed to tell Aunt Sally *not* to send you 'pogey bait.'"

He took Weezil into the hallway, I mean passageway, and sat him down on a lower step of the stairs, I mean ladder, going to the second deck.

"Open it!"

Weezil ripped off the cellophane and opened the box.

"Go ahead, Sweetie, have one."

"Sir, the private isn't *allowed* to have pogey bait!"

"No *shit*," Snake confirmed. "but this time it's all right. Go ahead, take a cherry."

Weezil took a cherry and popped it into his mouth.

"May I have a cherry, Sweetie," Snake asked playfully.

"Yes, sir," the brown nosing Weezil shouted, brightening.

Snake took the proffered cherry and placed it on the center of Weezil's head. Weezil's smile disappeared as Snake grabbed Weezil's wrist and placed his palm on top of the cherry.

Whapp! Snake slapped Weezil's hand, squashing the cherry on Weezil's burr head. Syrup squirted from under Weezil's hand.

"Your turn," Snake cooed.

Weezil ate another cherry.

"My turn," Snake sang excitedly and another cherry

was placed on Weezil's head. He positioned Weezil's hand over the cherry. Whapp! And another cherry joined the fate of the first.

And another. And another. Soon cherries and juice were streaming down Weezil's face and ears.

"Would you like another cherry, Sweetie," Snake cooed.

"No, sir," Weezil screamed. Had to admit it, the turd had balls.

"Oh, come on, Sweetie," Snake coaxed, "Aunt Sally would want you to enjoy the cherries that you were told *not* to have anyone send you. Have another cherry," he shouted.

"Aye, aye, sir," Weezil agreed miserably. He ate another cherry.

"Do you want another cherry, Sweetie," Snake asked sweetly.

"Yes, sir," Weezil shouted.

"Well it's *not your turn*, you goddammed glutton! Wouldn't Aunt Sally want you to share with your buddies?"

"Yes, sir," Weezil allowed.

Snake took another cherry. Another 'whapp!' soon followed. Weezil and Snake took turns eating and whapping the cherries until Snake took a quick step back from Weezil and folded his arms.

A torrent of water cascaded down the floor above, drenching Weezil. SSgt. Sword gazed placidly down from the second deck railing, holding an empty bucket.

Weezil was heard shortly thereafter requesting a head call in which he hung over a throne, giving back the contraband cherries.

CHAPTER 10 – REFLECTIONS

Happy Hour

My favorite time of the day, of course, was taps. At taps, the DIs released us from their clutches for seven beautiful, sweet, peaceful hours. Generally, I was so exhausted that I fell asleep immediately after wishing Chesty good night. I determined to stave off sleep for just a couple of minutes of day-dreaming therapy. I worked quickly through the day, omitting the times I had wimped out, screwed up, or got punished. I'd review how I had inserted food into my "crumb catcher" without missing my mouth, not an easy job when eating at attention with your eyes straight ahead. I'd recall how I put my left foot down after the right foot and how I had correctly known General Order No. 8; "To give the alarm in case of fire or disorder." These small successes helped build confidence.

Snake occupied most of my conscious thoughts. His smirking face appeared when I closed my eyes at night. His ridiculous cadence intruded in my ears when I ate lunch and dinner. I lived in constant fear that I would screw up again and owe him 4 thousand pushups, or that I was Gooney Bird's replacement. I was convinced that his two ounces of brain was working overtime to devise a way to trip me up. It occurred to me that he seemed determined for me to graduate posthumously.

He found more and more fault with me, baiting me with questions, hoping I would give some smartass answer. Like Dumbo and Gooney Bird, I was on Snake's shit list, a menace to the Corps, disrespectful of authority, a clown, a smartass. Sgt. Gibson seemed neutral on the issue but SSgt. Sword was in charge. *His* favorable opinion I had to have.

Let's see what Attaboys I had scored with SSgt.

Sword: one Awe Shit for bungling reading the prayer in the mess hall on the first day, and one Awe Shit for losing my brother's rear sight aperture on the parade ground on the third day. Zero for two. I vowed to try my hardest to stay in step, get a glossy shine on my shoes, and win my first Attaboy.

Next, I moved on to punishing Snake for intruding on my day in this Island Paradise, making him do pushups and giving him a few rabbit punches to the gut, to teach him a little respect. I asked him a simple Marine Corps History question like "what was Chesty Puller's dog's name?" Punishment, of course, for an incorrect answer. I advised him to get his hot, beady eyes off me and to get down for more pushups. Was he in love with me? Then, with a final goodnight to Chesty, I would drift off to sleep. Hopefully, Chesty would look after me one more day.

That night I dreamed of home; home, sweet, blessed, wonderfully boring home. I was having a Coke on the back porch; listening to the Pittsburgh Pirates beat up on the Chicago Cubs when two beefy Marine MPs charged onto the porch and dragged me screaming to an olive drab panel truck.

Instead of locking me up, they returned me to Parris Island where I was a drill instructor receiving a new platoon. As I walked along the ranks of my new charges I came upon a recruit that looked a lot like the Snake.

"What the hell's your name, turd," I barked.

"Sir, the recruit's name is Private Snake!"

Aha! It was Snake! He cringed as my eyes bored into his. I pinched his Adam's apple, just for the fun of it.

"I don't like you, turd," I pronounced. "You are the most miserable looking little shit I've seen since I've been a drill instructor."

I thought I detected a flicker of recognition in his

staring eyes.

"How in the hell did you get into my Corps? Was it reform school or the Corps? Surely no recruiter would have allowed you to voluntarily join my Corps? Get down and give me a hundred pushups!"

"I can't hear you, turd! Sound off! Are you a little girl, Snake?"

"No, sir," he screamed.

"You are gonna be my special project, Snake. You don't belong in my Marine Corps! I'll see you tonight at taps in front of my hatch. We're going to have a little personal instruction. You will dress in your field jacket, cartridge belt, canteen, rifle, mattress and locker box."

I smiled in my sleep with no penalty.

Getting To Know You

Our drill instructors' personalities emerged quickly.

SSgt. Sword never smiled and was all business. He was matter of fact; a teacher without remorse when delivering punishment. Nothing was personal, including crushing your Adam's apple or rabbit punching you in the gut. He looked you right in the eye with the message, "this is for your own good, private." It was his duty, as he saw it, to objectively pound the Corps' virtues and values into us, no matter how little pain it caused him. Sword seemed to force himself to use foul language and spoke the bad words with perfect diction, like he was trying them on.

Snake was a reptile of a different breed. He cackled with glee as he dished out punishment, thoroughly enjoying his work. He used foul language as though it was the mother tongue and was very creative in his swearing. He was the most imaginative of the three DIs and was always trying to set new records. He was our constant companion and probably volunteered for extra duty. His voice was a surprising baritone which he made even deeper when he taunted us. He lacked warmth.

Gibson loped along in a manner close enough to be called marching. He spoke with a Southern twang, maybe Tennessean. Unlike Sword and Snake, he never lowered his voice and always seemed to shout everything; he just yelled, fumed, and raged in his normal voice. He didn't seem to have a mean bone in his body, but neither did he cut us any breaks. He was kind of a big brother who was going to teach his little brother even if it killed him. Gibson was full of famous and homespun quotations and other pearls of wisdom.

Our sister platoon, 2038, lived upstairs, or topside. The poor devils of 2038 had inherited the undesirable Sgt. Frog. If the Corps had let us recruits do things in a democratic manner, like pick players on a pickup team, he would have been picked last. His high school yearbook probably said "Most likely to kick your ass."

I noticed the Marine Corps didn't have any calendars, or at least enough to pass out to us turds. Everything was more or less spontaneous. We never knew what was coming next; drill, swimming, classes, chow, shit, or go blind.

The lay of the land became more familiar. India Company and the remainder of the Second Battalion's barracks were lined up along a street across from our own mess hall. But, like in a prisoner of war camp, there were no street signs. I was lost every time we went more than a block in any direction.

My Fellow Turds

The days wore on and I began to get to know or know something about my fellow turds. We had lost eight of our original number and picked up seven recycled turds from the Fat Man's Platoon and Motivation. At first, each of us was just trying to survive without any thought as to who the guy was next to you doing pushups. We didn't trust anyone or want anyone to see that we may be on the verge of pulling a "Four Eyes."

There were two kinds of recruits; regulars and "reserves." Regulars had joined for either three or four years. Reserves had only a six-month active duty commitment, followed by years meeting once a month in the active reserves in their hometown. The DIs considered the Reserves to be slightly above the status of draft dodgers, but lower than whaleshit, and not in the real Corps.

Some of my fellow turds were reserves and the drill instructors constantly badgered them to become "real Marines" by voluntarily extending their enlistment. Some of these reserves were baseball players on the farm teams of major league baseball clubs. The great baseball player Roberto Clemente was reported to be undergoing training in one of the rival platoons. After the pushups, running, and physical abuse he was getting, he'd probably go back to his team and easily bat .750.

Turds joined the Corps for all sorts of reasons. Some had their choice of jail, reform school, or the Marines. Gooney Bird, from West Virginia was caught joyriding in a stolen car with his buddy. The judge, a former Marine, offered him the choice of six months in jail or six months in the Marine Corps. Both Gooney Bird and his buddy had accepted and were now fellow turds, for better or worse.

In the first week the Navy dentist had pulled every tooth out of Gooney Bird's head, forcing him to gum his meals. It also slurred his speech into "yeth, thurh" instead of "yes, sir." He hummed constantly to make up for his loss of speech; while cleaning his rifle, shining shoes; even while marching. At times it sounded more like a dog whining to get out to do his business, but no one had the heart to tell him to knock it off. I guess we were all silently whining.

The drill instructors had apparently decided Gooney Bird would not make a good Marine, and called him to their hut nightly for pushups and other extra physical instruction. Sometimes they no sooner released him from a bout of punishment when they called him right back for another dose. Gooney Bird was run so ragged that he often cried on his way back from their hut.

Because Gooney Bird was so much garbage, he was consigned to the GI can during field day inspections. He crawled into the GI can, pulled the lid on top of him. When the lid was tapped, he interrupted his humming and reported "all garbage present and accounted for."

Gooney Bird had two left feet, got his thumb caught in the bolt of his rifle on inspection arms, couldn't remember military rank structure, his general orders, or how to take his rifle apart, let alone get it back together again. Gooney Bird caught more flack from the DIs than any ten other turds. He wasn't just any turd; he was the turds' turd. In an effort to hide in his shadow, I did my best to be near him at all times.

But Gooney Bird's West Virginia buddy, also at Parris Island courtesy of the Charleston, West Virginia police authorities, stuck by him. Gooney and his buddy were thicker than thieves, which in fact, they both were.

Even though the rest of the platoon had done many extra pushups because Gooney Bird had constantly screwed up, almost none wanted to see him get the boot. Maybe because we didn't want to become the new target. Some of his fellow turds helped him spitshine his shoes, clean his rifle, and when the DIs weren't looking, pushed him over the obstacles at the physical training obstacle course. One turd even whispered 'left-right, left-right' for Gooney while we marched.

The only contribution I could make to help Gooney in his misery was to share a quotation I had read in a book about Winston Churchill. "Never, ever, ever, ever, give up!

Never give up!" Gooney asked if Churchill had gone through Parris Island. I told him that Churchill had had his own island problem but he had made it through.

Another fugitive from justice, and according to Hoot, the result of lusty, unplanned sex, was Private Spyder. Spyder was the last of several classmates in line to pollonize the class Rosie Rottencrotch in the girls' bathroom at his high school. The drill instructors promptly named him "Stud."

Some of the turds who got the choice of jail or the Corps were sent to the Motivation Platoon, where every turd was a badass and needed "motivation" to get with the program. In this homey little platoon, everybody beat the shit out of everybody else until they got tired of disagreeing with the system. To be sent to Motivation was to be sent to hell.

Then we had Randazzo, who was unhappy with boot camp and tried to think of ways to escape. He took to asking to go to sick call every day. Everyday he was asked if he was too sick to have sex with Rosie Rottencrotch. He admitted he was never too sick to have sex. Since having sex took physical stamina, it followed that he then must be able to march and do pushups. Request denied.

Randazzo was confident that he could get a "get out of Parris Island Free Card." He bragged that he would soon be singing "Happy Trails to You" to Snake and the rest of us with a farewell chorus of "so long, suckers."

Randazzo then tried to get out by eating broken light bulbs and razor blades. When that didn't work, he climbed up on the second floor banister and threatened to jump. Snake went up to try to talk him down. After pronouncing him a rotten little motherfucker, Randazzo jumped, from the banister to the second story floor, and crouched in a corner. He proceeded to make sounds that he said were like a carrot, until the Navy POU people came to get him. Randazzo gave me a "so long, suckers" wink as the Navy Corpsmen took him away in a tight fitting white coat with no arms.

About three weeks into the training, two nervous Navy Shore Patrolmen showed up at our barracks. They entered our squadbay with SSgt. Sword and we were ordered to attention in front of our racks. I observed with an inward smile that the two SPs snapped to attention for a moment before they allowed themselves to slack off to embarrassed rigid stances of interested onlookers.

"Private Connors," Sword barked, "get your sorry ass up here!"

Private Connors, a five-foot-four turd from the Little End, ran up to the drill instructor and stood frozen at attention.

"Or is it *Seaman* Connors," Sword challenged.

"Sir, *Private* Connors!"

"You are not Seaman Aloysius X. Connors, AWOL from the Navy?"

"Sir," Connors insisted, "Private Connors is a *Marine*!"

"Wait outside," Sword instructed the two SPs. They wasted no time getting outside.

"Connors," Sword lectured, "you can't just quit the Swabbies because they're an inferior service. You went AWOL, you dumb shit! You got a death wish?"

"Sir, the private is not AWOL! The private is serving in the Marine Corps!"

"It's the first goddammed time I ever saw a Swabbie hiding in the Marine Corps." Sword mused. "Maybe you're making a career of attending boot camps. Are you going to try the Army next? Do you want to stay in the Corps?"

"Sir, the private does," Connors persisted.

"Get down and give me twenty pushups for being so dammed dumb to join the Swabbies!" Sword went out to tell the SPs.

Another fugitive was Private Turnbee. This time it was the civilian police that showed up.

"Turnbee, are you married," Sword demanded.

"Sir, the private is," Turnbee stammered, "sort of!"

"What the hell is 'sort of'? You're either married or you're not!"

"Sir, the private is getting divorced!"

"He skipped before the judge could award his wife alimony," One of the cops interjected. "I have a warrant for him. He comes with us." He reached for Turnbee's shoulder.

"No, he doesn't," Sword advised, pulling the cop's hand off Turnbee's shoulder, "you're on a federal reservation. You have no authority here. We'll take care of it."

The two cops looked at each other, shrugged, and handed over the paperwork. As they left the barracks, I thought they were damned lucky that Sword didn't order them to drop to the deck and deliver twenty pushups.

"Turnbee, you dumb shit," Sword turned to berate Turnbee, "you better not marry anybody else before you get this squared away! You're too young to get married. Besides, you're married to the Marine Corps! Get down and give me twenty!"

The far majority of turds weren't in trouble with the law. They were simply the Boy Next Door, eighteen or nineteen years old, high school graduates, some with some college, just trying to make their way to maturity.

Primarily because his name was alphabetically closest to mine, Glenn W. Johnson, a.k.a. Buffalo Butt, shared the double decker rack I slept in. Buffalo Butt was also good at the high jump and could get in top rack with a springing leap. The Butt tried hard to make the program and was very nervous about doing things right without any deviation, such as shaving improperly or eating noisily at the chow hall. You didn't get sent back to Georgia for not making the grade. He didn't understand Darrell Dottle either, and continuously repeated "left, right, left right" in his head, ignoring Snake's so called cadence. This approach didn't work either.

Being from Saltpeter, Georgia, he was lucky to be born at all. Buffalo had a dominating girlfriend named Scarlett Buttlett. Miss Buttlett was his advisor, lecturer and resident Snake at Home. I suspected she corresponded with Snake for ways to keep him in line in the future.

Buffalo Butt became my closest friend and confidante.

The constant reference to us recruits as "turds" became a familiar and comfortable label. It wasn't until much later that I found out that "Turd" was supposedly an acronym for "Trainee Under Rapid Development." I'm sure that was the spirit in which the DIs referred to us, like in "cadet." Yeah, right.

CHAPTER 11 – WHO GOES THERE?

No Fire or Disorder That I Can See

That night I had my first Fire Watch.

To be assigned Fire Watch was to lose two hours of precious sleep. The official uniform for the job was utilities, cartridge belt with canteen, cover, and tennis shoes. It was an easy but boring task. You walked the rectangle of the squadbay, quietly in your tennis shoes, keeping an eye out for fire and disorder, or bats and shit flying around the squadbay.

The only creature stirring that night was a grey mouse but I didn't really think I should report him. I watched him for a while and decided that he wasn't causing any problems or disorder. He probably even outranked me. I challenged him, but he ignored me and passed without proper authority. He must take days off and do his PT and marching only at night. What did he eat? I felt sorry for him for having to spend his whole life in boot camp, never to graduate. Maybe I should have "run him up," or reported him, for impersonating a turd.

Our orders were also to watch for turds trying to bunk with each other, read letters or Marine Corps Handbooks with their flashlights under the blanket (singular), or other such outrages. The sounds of snoring broke the otherwise still night. One temperature fits all, no fooling with the thermostat, if there was one. No extra blankets or tucking in your buddy. No pajamas with feet.

I wondered if Chesty had called it a night somewhere, or was out cracking up streets with tanks and installing beer machines. My kind of guy. I decided that Chesty had hit the rack and that the safety of the civilized world was now up to me. What would Chesty do on Fire Watch? He would, of course, perform his military duty efficiently and fearlessly. Ahhh, fearlessly!

I, too, would fearlessly stomp along my assigned beat and pounce on any disorder. Chesty would also fearlessly face the Drill Instructors' wrath. Chesty would march with confidence, do a thousand pushups if necessary, flex his Adam's apple, and smile. Piece of cake. If only I could be a tiny bit like Chesty. I resolved to borrow a small piece of Chesty to get through the next weeks. I won't let you down, Chesty. I wondered if I was taking too big of a liberty. Naw, Chesty was out for the troops. He wouldn't mind. I straightened my shoulders, took a deep breath, flexed my Adam's apple, and fearlessly swaggered toward the end of the squadbay.

Sleep Walk

I leaned against the window, officially called a "porthole," and looked out at the concrete wash racks. I half expected to see blazing spotlights from watchtowers sweeping across the barracks doors and compound. I wondered if a tunnel up to and under the main gate was possible when my reverie was interrupted by Dumbo mumbling in his sleep.

"Aye, aye, sir! Yes, sir!" His muttering became louder as he became more agitated.

"Aye, aye, sir," he screamed. "2037! Get outside!"

"2037, get outside," a dozen or so turds echoed and bedlam ensued. Turds bounded out of their racks, donned their flip flops, and headed toward the hatch.

This surely came under the purview of disorder and, according to my orders, I was to give the alarm.

"Wait, wait," I tried to keep my voice down,

grabbing the arms of running turds, "it was only Dumbo talking in his sleep." But no one would stop. Not even Dumbo, who himself passed several turds as he headed for the street.

In less than ten seconds, I was standing alone in the squadbay. No sound ensued from the drill instructor's hut. Every swinging dick was on the street. The platoon was in three ranks, automatically performing the "dress, right, dress" maneuver. They dropped their arms and froze at attention, the guidon with his flagless pole in his position.

Seventy-three turds, dressed only in T-shirts and skivvy shorts, stood at attention in their flip-flops on a chilly October morning, ready to do pushups or march to Pretoria, if ordered.

I ran outside and up to the Section Leader, King of the Turds. I felt a little guilty being warmly dressed and being out of uniform with my fellow turds.

"We gotta get them back inside. That was only Dumbo talking in his sleep. He was the one that yelled 'get outside.' The drill instructor is still sleeping."

"Shit! Well, we can't just go back. What if he wakes up and asks why the hell we're running night exercises on our own? No, we have to stay here until he tells us to get inside."

"I told you, he's still asleep. He doesn't know we're out here. We could just sneak in."

"You're the fire watch. Do something!"

"I'm fire watch of the *squadbay*," I reminded him, hiding behind my general orders. Streets don't catch on fire.

Still, I thought about telling them to get their asses inside. Halfway there, Hoot would wake up and ask me if I thought I was a general. No, I wasn't going to do that.

"Go in and wake him up," the King of the Turds

suggested, "tell him we're out here."

"You mean pound on the pine? I'll wake everybody up. They're not supposed to get us up before reveille. There'll be big trouble."

"I don't give a shit how you get him up. Just get him up! It's damned cold out here."

"But..."I started.

"Get him *up*, goddammit! You want your own blanket party? I'm the Section Leader and I'm telling you to get him up!"

"Okay," I agreed, now that I had an official order and the threat of a visit from the Night People, "I'll do it."

I plodded silently on my sneakers into the barracks and up to the drill instructor's hut. What to do? If I pounded on the pine, the drill instructors in the next hut would hear and turn Hoot in for falling out his platoon at 0300.

If I went into his hut, forbidden ground, and shook him by the shoulder, he'd likely go into a combat stance and stab me with the bayonet he probably kept under his pillow.

I knocked softly three times on the transom. Nothing. I eased up to the hatch and peered in. Hoot was on his back snoring. I stepped back and rapped a little harder. Hoot continued snoring. I rapped a little harder. No result. I rapped a lot harder.

Hoot snorted and rolled over.

"Sir," I whispered, "sir!"

"What? Whatsis," he mumbled.

"Sir, it's Private Joyce, the fire watch."

"What the hell? What time is it? What's the matter?" The rack springs screeched.

"Sir, it's 0300 and the platoon is outside on the street."

"What? What did you say? Jesus Christ!" He ran to the window and saw 2037 manning the street. "What the hell are they doing out there?"

"Sir, a recruit talks in his sleep and he yelled '2037, get outside.'"

"Jesus fuckin' Christ! Judas fuckin' Priest!" He pulled his trousers on.

"Get out there. Tell them no talking, no noise. I'll be right out. Quietly!"

"Aye, aye, sir." I whispered.

I walked quickly outside and told the Section Leader. No talking, no noise.

Hoot appeared almost immediately, hesitated a moment when he saw the skivvy brigade, then resumed his stride to the Section Leader.

"No noise," he put his forefinger to his lips. "Okay, listen up," he said, keeping his voice low, "when I give the word, I want you to fall out and get into the barracks. Don't bang the door and don't jump into your racks. Quietly. Okay, get inside."

"2037, get inside," the platoon shouted automatically, the now ingrained response plus "I can't *hear* you" taking over. But to a man, they tippy-toed their way into the squadbay and carefully and noiselessly climbed into their racks.

Lights flashed on as Hoot stood alone on the street, dumbfounded.

Two minutes later, a car pulled up and Hoot got to entertain the Officer of the Day. The car was still there an hour later when I was relieved of fire watch.

Nod if You Agree

The next morning Hoot called the platoon together for a little lecture. I was excused to make a head call. I was not eager to rejoin the turds and took my time. Perhaps too much time.

"Well, no shit, Private Joyce has generously decided to honor us with his presence. Is it convenient for you to participate in the program?"

"Yes, Sir!"

Were you having a shit hemorrhage in there?"

"No, Sir!"

"Maybe you'd like us to start without you?"

"No, Sir!"

"Maybe you'd like to run the program?" Did he think I had the platoon fall out last night?

"No, Sir!"

"Bullshit, tell them to get down for pushups!"

I was so used to screaming "No, Sir" that I almost disobeyed the order. Finally I yelled for them to get down for pushups and they immediately fell to the deck.

"Well, are you going to let them fall asleep on the deck or are you going to get them going?"

"One," I yelled and my fellow turds pushed up from the floor. "Two!" and they sank back to the floor.

After twenty pushups I looked at Gibson. He looked at me. I thought I detected a slight nod.

"Okay, turds," I barked, "on your feet!"

Instantly Hoot was in my face.

"Who in the hell told you to have them stop? What the hell do you think you're doing? Did I tell you to have them stop?"

His nose almost touched the top of my head and his spit dotted on my forehead. Although he was in my face, the situation didn't seem to require me to tense the muscles of my Adam's apple in anticipation of getting grabbed in the throat.

"Sir, the private thought the drill instructor nodded his head for the private to stop the pushups and…"

"Don't beat around the bush, you sonofabitch; just tell me straight. What're you got, shit for brains?"

Well, no, Sarge, I thought sarcastically, not unless my digestive track is upside down.

"The private is full of shit! The private isn't supposed to think! I'm the one that's paid to think! I'm the one that tells you when to shit, how much and what color! Do you understand?"

"Yessir, the private understands!"

"No, you don't," Hoot argued, shaking his head, "set a beggar on horseback and he rides at a gallop. Get down for pushups."

"No," he turned to the turds, "just Private Smartass. The rest of you will just nod."

"Aye, aye, Sir," the turds screamed, nodding up and down like a flock of pecking chickens.

I labored through a couple of dozen or so pushups while my fellow turds nodded solemnly.

"Well, turds," Hoot demanded, "shall we allow Private Smartass get to his feet?"

The confused turds did not answer. Any answer, they knew, would be the wrong answer. They just kept nodding because they hadn't been told to stop nodding.

Hoot began nodding too. "Well, everyone seems to

think you should stop. But you won't stop," he thundered, "just because some people are nodding! Half of these people are probably just falling asleep for Chrissake! Don't you agree, Private Smartass?"

"Twenty-eight, two, sir!" I interrupted my count. "Yes, sir! Twenty-nine, two, sir!"

"You are a fast learner, Private Smartass. Now watch my head. Shall you quit doing pushups and get to your feet?" He nodded twice, slowly and deliberately.

I hesitated in my count. Sure as hell looked like a "Yes, get on your feet." On the other hand, was a nod a lawful order even if I wanted it to be? Up till now all our commands had been verbal, although I supposed a drill instructor could do almost anything. They had arm and hand signals for patrols, didn't they? I decided to wait for one of the official arm and hand signals.

"Thirty-one, two, sir," I continued, "thirty-two, two, sir!"

Hoot studied me, his poker face not giving anything away.

"Don't you want to get up?" He leaned down to look into my face.

"Yes, sir, but the drill instructor did not instruct the private through verbal or accepted arm and hand signal for the private to do so. Thirty-five, two, sir."

"You're goddammed right I *didn't* order you to get up, Private Smartass. You may have finally learned something. Even a blind pig noses up an acorn once in a while. On your feet!"

I gratefully jumped to my feet and stood at ramrod attention.

Hoot whipped his hand, palm down, at the floor. "Hit the dirt," he screamed. Seventy-four bodies instantly hugged the floor.

"Ahhh, good," he smiled. "This is getting to be fun. On your feet! Hit the dirt! Yes, that's very good."

Hoot turned to the prone turds. "Who in the hell told you people to quit nodding? Ain't no fuckin' hope for you people! Gimme twenty more pushups! I didn't tell you to quit nodding."

A smattering of thumps and bumps ensued as the nodding turds clunked their heads on the floor on the downside of their pushup.

"I don't have to pound the shit out of your heads. Turds, you do it to yourselves. This'll be the only platoon in history that the Corps had to issue helmets to so they could do pushups."

People in India are Starving

Guard duty was only a one-day affair. My post was at the mess hall, behind the GI can on the way out of the hall, complete with cartridge belt, canteen, bayonet, and a nightstick.

My job was to prevent turds from throwing away edible government property. Before exiting the mess hall, all recruits had to scrape off their trays and stack them on a shelf in a little scullery window. I ensured that they did not scrape off any horsecock or SOS into the can, thereby costing the Corps needless bucks from the chow budget.

Before morning chow, SSgt. Sword marched Buffalo Butt and me to the mess hall and posted us at opposite ends of the hall.

"Stand behind the GI can," Sword advised, "and hold the nightstick like so."

He gripped the nightstick in his right hand, tapping the end menacingly in his left palm.

"The only things that go into this can are bones and paper. No mashed potatoes, no meat. Only bones and paper. Understand?"

I said I understood, although I never saw any turds reading newspapers. Seemed simple enough.

"If they try to get through here with food, you will point them to one of the tables near the hatchway and instruct them to finish the food. The refuse in the can shouldn't get above this level."

He tapped the can with the nightstick about one-fourth the distance from the bottom.

"Do you know the procedure for the nightstick as outlined in the Guidebook for Marines section on the use of weapons while assigned to Interior Guard?"

"Yes, sir!"

"Well," he sighed, shifting his feet, "are you going to *tell* me?"

"Sir, a sentry will confine the use of the nightstick to that portion of the body below the shoulders. The head will not be struck except in a last resort to protect human life!"

It hardly seemed likely that two recruits would be locked in a fight to the death over some tube steak. Nor did I really expect a turd with some uneaten carrots to attack me on the way out the door.

"That's right. Try not to kill anyone. What's your first general order?"

"Sir, to take charge of this post and all government property in view!"

"You will remain at the post until the last recruit at evening chow has eaten and left. You will then report to my hatch at the barracks. Understood?"

"Yes, sir!"

And then he was off and I was on my own, a responsible member of America's security forces in charge of the post. I could see into the mess hall and also into the kitchen from the post. If it's in view, I'm in charge, my general orders stated.

In that case, why don't we have steak tonight? Maybe some pie, too. Let them eat cake. Let's hand out a little government property to the turds.

While I was surveying my domain, the first wave of recruits marched into the hall and sidestepped their way down the chow line. I kept a sharp eye on possible violators, tapping my nightstick authoritatively against my palm. Don't fool with me, turds.

Don't take so much; I silently admonished the smaller turds. You can't eat all that. Well, you're not getting out of here unless you choke it all down. It's my duty to protect against uneaten food. People in India are starving.

The gulpers were already rising from the tables and heading toward my post. Ahhh, some customers!

As the first recruit approached, I made a show of looking at his tray, tapping my stick. It was clean as a whistle; the turd must have licked it clean. Good man, carry on, turd. Place your tray in the window and get your skuzzy ass outa here.

The next recruit had a chunk of uneaten bread on his tray.

"You'll have to sit over there," I advised, pointing with my Interior Guard weapon, "and finish off the bread."

He stuffed the bread in his mouth and bolted while I nodded my official approval. He deposited the tray and ran out the door.

A few more offending recruits hastily shoved the remains of their meals in their mouths rather than sit at the tables. As long as they didn't fill up my GI can, I couldn't see as how my insisting that they sit down and eat like gentlemen instead of gluttons made much difference.

I knew from first hand experience what being late from chow entailed. After the chewing out and perhaps a few pushups, you had to run around the platoon as it marched to its next destination. For every hundred paces the platoon marched, you ran about a quarter of a mile. If you were running to PT, or physical training, you were exhausted before you started.

A new challenge showed up. A small thin recruit in brand new utilities, complete with tags, tried to scrape off half a tray of government property.

"You'll have to eat that over there," I advised the turd.

"I can't eat it, man," he whined, "I'm sick."

"You have to finish your tray," I repeated, "why did you take so much?"

"They kept putting it on. I can't, man," he pleaded. "I gotta get outside!"

I briefly thought about tapping him with the billy club a couple of times in that portion of the body below the shoulders but, to tell you the truth, I felt sorry for him.

I looked at the bottom of the GI can. Not too much, I decided. What the hell, this guy does look sick. Probably scared sick. I looked around for SSgt. Sword; all clear.

"Don't take so much next time. Hold your tray back if you don't want anymore. Get rid of it and get outa here."

"Thanks, buddy," he said sincerely, "thanks a lot!"

Well, I was in charge, right? This was my post and I was the one who decided what was best for the Corps and the property in view. It was better to have a healthy recruit than salvage a lump of food of dubious nutritional value. It was a command decision.

Noon chow came and went without incident. I had settled into my routine and had nothing to report. An irritating distraction, however, was the constant ringing of the mess sergeant's phone. The sergeant seemed to be on it constantly in a series of short conversations. Maybe he was taking reservations.

I imagined SSgt. Sword calling Dodge City's finest house of cuisine. "Yes, party of seventy-four, please. Yes, we will all have the blue plate special, the Flaming Fillet of Yak, Peking Style." Whatever cut of yak or goat or possum they would be serving would look like it was charred by a flamethrower.

The sound of hungry turds arriving for their evening yak broke into my thoughts. It was back to safeguarding the leftovers of the latest culinary triumph. The turds having seen me in action during the morning and noon chow, knew me to be a tough but compassionate sentry. They gobbled their chow and did not waste much of the Corps' vittles.

A familiar recruit approached; one I had talked with on the train down to Yemassee.

"Hey man, how's it goin," he asked.

"Good," I said, "how 'bout you?"

"This is really some shit, hunh," he laughed, "just what the recruiting sergeant promised!"

"Yeah, right." I agreed.

Right then another face appeared directly in front of mine. A corporal in starched khakis glared back at me.

"What's your seventh general order, private?" Holy shit!

"Sir, to talk to no one except in the line of duty!"

"Were you laughing in the line of duty," he barked.

"Sir!" Sonofabitch had me there. I couldn't say the turd and I were laughing about cleaning his tray.

"When you are relieved, you will report to your drill instructor that you violated your seventh general Order!"

He turned and strode out of the mess hall before I could say another word. The laughing turd had also vanished.

Now I had a problem. My sixth general order was "To receive, obey, and pass on to the sentry who relives me all orders from the commanding officer, officer of the day, and officers and non-commissioned officers of the guard only."

This guy wasn't an officer or non-commissioned officer of the guard. He sure as hell wasn't the commanding officer or officer of the day. Therefore, I couldn't legally receive any orders from him. Since I had already quit laughing, I didn't have any orders to obey. I wasn't going to be relieved by another sentry so had nothing to pass on.

On the other hand, the Corporal was probably the drill instructor's brother. Or his drinking buddy. They would have a big laugh at the NCOs Club over their beers. But would SSgt. Sword think it funny if I hadn't told him? Disobedience of a direct order!

If I reported that I was having a goddammed tea party on guard duty, Sword would fry my ass. If I didn't tell him and the other troublemaker told him, I'd be in really deep shit.

The end of chow came and went and Buffalo Butt and I slowly marched back to the barracks. The Butt, of course, being the tight ass that he is, thought I should immediately report to Sword and sing like a canary. I agonized over the dilemma, occasionally hitting my body with the nightstick, below the shoulders as prescribed. I figured a little preparatory punishment would help me to get warmed up for what was coming.

I pounded on the pine at the Drill instructor's hatch.

"Speak," Sgt. *Snake* bellowed.

Oh, no, please, not Snake. Where the hell was Sword?

"Sir, Private Joyce reporting as ordered!"

"Get your ass in here!" Holy shit! He knew!

I marched into the drill instructor's hut and stood at attention.

"Did you complete your duty at the chow hall as ordered?"

"Yes, sir!"

He gazed at me and he knew. He walked slowly around me, keeping his eyes on my face.

"Do you have something to report, turd, or do you always looks like somebody stole your teddy bear?" Observant sonofabitch.

"Sir, someone gave the private an unlawful order!" There, I had said it.

"*Who* the hell gave you an order," Snake bellowed, "what did he say?"

"Sir, a corporal told me to report upon relief to my drill instructor that the private had violated his seventh general order!"

"What did he look like," Snake demanded, "was he a drill instructor?"

"He was dressed in starched khakis, sir! The private doesn't think he was a drill instructor, sir!"

"Come with me," Snake rasped and strode out of the room.

We practically double-timed it back to the mess hall, which was now deserted except for the mess hall crew.

Snake quickly searched the entire hall with me in close pursuit, but thankfully, no joy in Turdville.

Snake appeared to be furious that another Marine presumed to give one of his turds an order. Although I knew him to be a sadistic sonofabitch capable of all kinds of punishment, I had never seen him as pissed as he was at the unknown corporal who had messed with his turd.

He was so pissed that after a quick march home to the barracks, he forgot to grill me about violating my seventh general order.

The Eyes of Platoon 2037 Are Upon You

Besides Protector of Uneaten Food and Firewatch, another responsible position I sometimes held was Clothesline Watch. After the turds washed and hung their clothes, I walked around the back yard to make sure no one stole the clothes. The local black market didn't seem to have much of a demand for wet soap stained clothing so this duty, too, was fairly boring.

Once a turd from our sister platoon had clothesline watch at the same time I did. Although we weren't allowed to talk except in the line of duty, he told me that his DI Frog could kick my DI's ass. Thinking of Snake, I hoped so, too, but told him my DI could flip the Frog three times in the air before be hit the deck. Snake was a mean little shit, but he was *our* mean little shit.

Sometimes it rained but the security conscious DIs insisted that the soggy clothes still be protected. If it rained before you went on duty you got to wear a poncho. If it rained in the middle of your watch you didn't wear a poncho. Since nature had issued you the perfect raincoat, the human skin, a poncho was just an added luxury. On the other hand, the rain rinsed out the soap stains and made our utilities rain water soft. Small comfort for duty as a walking human lightning rod.

Next to the wash racks was the drill instructors' parking lot. I noted that SSgt. Sword drove a 1957 mint green Chevy, the coolest car in the world, and Hoot had a shiny black 1949 Ford pickup. Snake drove a faded red Ford Falcon, which he understandably generally parked down the road.

Human lightning rod in poncho. The clothesline watch is at the center of the picture. Photo courtesy of Eugene Alvarez.

You can learn a lot about people just by reading their bumper stickers. For example, Hoot had a rifle and two stickers on the back window of his truck. NASCAR and NRA. Not the kind of guy you want to cut off at an intersection.

Snake also had two stickers, one a smiling sun from Myrtle Beach and the other from the base karate association. The message I got was "Please kick sand in my face."

SSgt. Sword had only one sticker: a USMC decal. Message: "It's all about the Corps."

One day I saw Snake's Falcon chug into the adjoining parking lot. A thin young woman with stringy hair got out of the passenger side and slid behind the wheel. After a lengthy admonition, Snake handed over command of the car to her and watched to see if she handled the car in a military manner. She eased off, stopping smoothly at the corner as she made her way out of the barracks area. As soon as he turned towards the barracks, I could hear the screech of tires as she floored it. My kind of girl.

Completing the platoon's security forces were the Road Guards. Normally, only the turds from the Big End were chosen for this duty and I was chosen only once. The road guards were sent out each time the platoon crossed an intersection, alley, or goat path to prevent merging vehicles from running down the marching turds. One particularly rainy day, a road guard waded out into the flooded street, tripped and momentarily disappeared from view. Only the bigger turds were considered capable of facing down an oncoming dump truck, tank, or your occasional submarine.

CHAPTER 12 – THESE ARE THE TIMES THAT TRY MENS SOLES

Just Go Ahead and Have a Big Tea Party

Other than when on the Night Train To Yemassee, or a few moments during our 30-minute "free-time" activity at night, I never had much of a chance to socialize.

We were always marching, exercising, or in class. In our so-called "free-time" we were busy cleaning our rifles or rubbing linseed oil on the stocks, shining our shoes, writing letters, or receiving "individual instruction" from the DI.

It was a tradeoff: shine shoes, clean rifles, or write letters. Shooting the shit was not an option unless you shot it with your fellow turds while doing one of the three. If you spent too much time writing letters, your shoes and rifle would suffer, followed a short time later with your suffering. If you spent all of your time shining and cleaning, the DI would haul you in because Mom would ask why she hadn't heard from Ole Skip. The DI would then think up some misery to encourage Ole Skip to pen a few words home.

We had been told that a rusty rifle was a court martial offense so that was the most important. Clean your rifle first. Next, the lack of shiny shoes caused the most problems. If there was time, next came writing letters, as long or short as time permitted. I solved the problem of letters to Mom, Dad, Baby Sister, and Little Bro and Aunt Grace by putting all their names on the same letter. This left other days for Wild Thing, Petunia, Kim, Chastity and Prudence.

My brother, US Caliber .30, M1, was easy to clean and took only a few minutes. Once or twice he got a snoot full of light powdery rust but that was easily taken care of with a toothbrush and oily rag.

Rubbing linseed oil on his wooden stock, however, seemed to be a never-ending task with no discernable results. It was tremendously boring, but I applied it lovingly, pretending I was putting suntan oil on Kim Novak's back. Poor Kim would have had to peel off the amount I put on, though. But my rifle was my brother, my best friend. Nothing was too good for my brother.

We were issued dress shoes early in the program. Although we wouldn't be wearing them until we got our green wool dress uniforms, we had a monumental amount of work to do on them to get the glossy shine. We did something called spit-shine. This involved rubbing a small amount of Kiwi dark brown shoe polish on the shoe with a T-shirt. You dipped a finger, tightly wound in a T-shirt, in some cold water in the lid of the Kiwi can, then made loving circular motions on the shoe. The water smoothed out the polish and, after hours of caressing the shoe, built a delicate smooth shell of polish, particularly on the toe.

One of our toothbrushes was sacrificed to apply polish to the outer soles and heels and the stitching between the soles and upper shoe. The outer soles and heels were also spit shined.

Depending on your technique, or the lack thereof, the shoes would obtain the desired glossy look or stubbornly resist, resulting in dull, murky, cloudy finishes. If our shoes did not glisten as the results of spit shine, the drill instructor would clinically inspect the shine and prescribe "more water" or "more polish" or "more work." The diagnosis "more work" also resulted in more pushups.

Every day the DIs would inspect not only our rifles and the dress shoes which we hoped to wear someday, but also our shave, equipment, and sometimes our locker boxes.

Writing, cleaning, and shining.
Photo courtesy of United States Marine Corps.

If our faces showed any hint of stubble, the DI would instruct us to "stand closer to the razor" and prescribe pushups to register the infraction in our memory.

I took some small satisfaction in insulting the DIs in some of my letters by understating what was going on. "Dear Mom: Things have been going very well. It gets a little boring with marching, physical training and classes. The weather is fine though, and our DI thought he might take us to the beach or swimming at the pool. I had a wonderful meal at the mess hall. Maybe my next duty station will be more of a challenge." It was great fun kidding myself, but I never sent the letter.

Individual, more accurately remedial, instruction also interfered with our social life during "free-time." The drill instructors, especially Sgt. Snake, would remember even minor infractions that we had committed during the day, or the day before, and call us to their hatch. Sometimes so many of us were called to the DIs hatch that we almost had to take a number.

My crimes were that I was guilty of eyeballing the area while at attention, getting out of step, and smiling. Smiling was my biggest offense, although I probably got caught at it only ninety percent of the time. When some unfortunate turd got reamed by a drill instructor in particularly humorous terms, I couldn't keep from smiling. That was what humor was, wasn't it?

Smile and the Whole World Doesn't Smile With You

One evening while I was greasing down Kim Novak, I heard Snake yell from his hatch.

"Joyce!"

"Private Joyce, Sir," the turds bellowed, relieved that it was not one of them.

"Get your ass in here!"

"Private Joyce, report to the drill instructor," they shouted. I guess you *can* teach turds new tricks.

I returned my best friend to the rifle rack, wiped my hands, and ran to Snake's hut. Standing in front of his hatch, I pounded on the pine.

"I can't *hear* you," jeered the Snake.

Then how the hell do you know I'm *out* here?

I almost broke my knuckles on his damn doorframe. I briefly considered kicking the wall to increase the sound to the level of his chronic sub-par hearing.

"Get your ass in here!"

I advanced three steps, bringing my heels together and stood at attention.

"Private Joyce reporting to the drill instructor as ordered, Sir!"

"Well, no shit, Joyce," he huffed, "you took your sweetass old time getting here! Are you free tonight? Am I interrupting something?"

"No, sir!"

"Were you smiling on the parade ground today, turd?" Snake switched gears.

"Sir...." Hell, did he see me or not? Accusations I can understand; questions gave too damned much latitude.

"Well, speak up," he badgered. "Yes? No? The drill instructor's a fucking liar? What?"

He *had* seen me. Should have confessed right off.

"Sir, the private was smiling!"

"You think learning to march is *funny*?"

I had an insane urge to tell him that yes, his cadence was incredibly funny, but he'd probably judo chop me twenty times or so, and follow it up by biting me in the neck.

"You have no *right* to be happy in boot camp." he continued, "were you having a good time out there, fucking up by the numbers?"

"No, Sir!"

"You had *better not* be! Get your weapon and get back here!"

I aye, ayed, got my rifle, and scurried back to his hut. Snake was waiting in the passageway outside his hatch.

"Up and on shoulders! Begin!"

Holding my brother, U. S. Rifle, Caliber .30, M1, with both hands at shoulder height, I began the exercise "by the numbers."

On Count One, I pushed the rifle straight up above my head. Two, I pulled the rifle down behind my neck. Three, I pushed the rifle above my head again. And Four, I pulled the rifle down to the starting position in front of my chest.

"*One*, two, three, four! *Two*, two, three, four! *Three*, two, three, four!"

"I'll let you know when," Snake muttered and slithered back into his den.

I continued snapping the rifle up and down over my head and behind my head, counting off the number of repetitions. I could see down the short passageway into the squad room of the other ground floor platoon. They were also on free-time, busily cleaning, writing, and polishing. Some of them glanced up from time to time, watching me working with my brother, the lethal dumbbell.

As time went on, my 9 1/2 pound brother got heavier and the snapping movements became sluggish pushes and controlled drops. My muscles burned, and as it became harder to breath, I began to grunt the count.

"*Foortty* Seven, twooo, threeee, foourr!"

Snake couldn't see me around the hatch, probably sitting at his desk studying his dog-eared copy of the Marquis de Sade's *Handbook of Torture Techniques*.

Absently, I continued the count, but did not lift the rifle. Shocked by my lapse, I pushed up the rifle on the next count. But that brief rest felt so good! Maybe I could skip raising the rifle on every other count. Which I did for a while.

Then I got greedy. Why raise the rifle at all if Snake couldn't see me?

I continued to grunt out the verbal count, putting real inflection in the laborious and increasingly challenging physical exercise, which I was happily not doing.

"*Ninety-seven*", grunt, "two, three, four!" Pause. "*Ninety-eight*!" Pause. "Two, three!" Grunt. "Four!" pause.

Some of the observing turds began to snicker, watching my facial contortions and swaying body in the midst of this performance, and a couple even chuckled.

"*Ninety-nine*! Two," Grunt. "Three!" Pause. "Four!"

Snake's face darted around the corner of the hatch like a cobra strike.

"What the *hell's* going on," he demanded, glancing at me, then glaring down the passageway toward the other platoon, whose members were once again busily involved in cleaning, writing, and polishing.

Fortunately, I was on the fourth count, requiring the rifle to be directly in front of my chest. That it had been there for the last twenty 4-count repetitions was between my best friend and me alone.

"Is somebody out here throwing some kind of a goddammed *tea* party?" He transfixed me with his aiming squint.

"No, sir!" It always paid to be truthful. I had no tea.

"You had better not be *shittin'* me, private," he screamed, still not satisfied. "Get back in the squadbay and get ready for lights out!"

"Aye, aye, sir!"

My brother, U.S. Rifle, Caliber .30, M1, and I hauled our grateful butts back into the squadbay and kept a low profile until lights out.

Although our rifle was generally used for up and on shoulder, a selected few of us were treated to "up and on shoulder locker box." Since the box was full of clothing it was a lot heavier than my brother. Snake would run us through the entire manual of arms with the box. "Port locker box" was the worst position as the box had to be held straight out from your body. Right or left shoulder locker box was a lot easier. After you struggled to get the box up on your shoulder it just rested there. I dropped it a couple of times, but mercifully was not ordered to sleep with it.

Who's From Philly?

When I first wrote home I was feeling a little sorry for myself and stupidly leaked that the DIs were mean, foul-mouthed thugs who gave Martha and Everett's baby boy a hard time. An avalanche of letters arrived from Martha, Everett, Baby Sister, Little Brother and Aunt Grace, advising their plans to write the DI, our Congressman, the President, and the Humane Society. Mom was willing to pay ransom for her poor boy; Dad was making plans to travel to Parris Island to reach an understanding with Snake, while Baby Sister, Little Bro and Aunt Grace were going to work on the congressman, the President, and the Humane Society.

At about this time Dad received a letter from Smiling Jack, my recruiter, gushing about how proud Dad must be that his son Turd was in Parris Island. Dad sent him a short letter inviting Jack to inspect, at close hand from a catwalk, a giant molten steel vat on the night shift at the steel mill where he worked.

Snake was blissfully unaware that Dad was prepared to make him part of a bridge girder along with Smiling Jack. Maybe the folks at the Humane Society had some ideas about how to humanely, or inhumanely, their choice, dispose of a troublesome reptile that nobody wanted.

Letters to Wild Thing and her sisters took on a different tone. I could hardly say I was on the ropes or that the little wimp might get washed out. It could happen. It was a matter of pride. No, I had to bravely admit it was tough but fortunately, it wasn't anything I couldn't handle. I laid it on sufficiently that the girls would know what a hero I was, but I needed their support, good graces, and later, compassion. Definitely *compassion*.

Then the day came that I was dreading. Baby Sister had informed me that she had written Snake a letter pronouncing him a sadistic, mean turd himself, and to lay off her brother and his buddies. I was not to worry, though, as she had not mentioned names or signed it and had sent it to Grandma Bertha in Philadelphia for remailing.

Snake burst in the squadbay while we were shining our shoes.

"Standby, attention!"

"Who lives in Philadelphia," he demanded. Clever fellow must have looked at the postmark. He looked around the squadbay.

"I said, who lives in Philadelphia, goddammit!"

No one moved. No one owned up to it.

"Goddammit, somebody must live in Philadelphia! Arright, get in front of your racks! We will go around the squadbay and each turd will sing out the name of the city and state where they're from."

Okay, you turd" he yelled at the first turd at the end of the squadbay, "where're you from?!

"Sir, Bangor, Maine!"

"You", he pointed to the next turd in line.

"Sir, Baltimore, Maryland!"

"Sir, Little Crotch Mountain, Pennsylvania!"

"Sir, Cleve- "the next turd began.

"Hold it! Hold it," Snake screamed. "You! Where is Little Crotch Mountain?" He stepped in front of the turd.

"Sir, it's in the middle of the state. There isn't any place near it!"

"Goddammit, there has to be someplace near it. What's the next town?"

146

"Sir, *Big* Crotch Mountain," the flustered turd yelled.

"Are you a fucking clown, turd," Snake threatened. I couldn't help suppress a smile.

"Joyce, get your ass up here!" I got my ass up there. "You think this is funny, turd?" He grabbed my Adam's apple. "Well, do you?"

"Sir, no, sir," I lied.

"Get down and give me twenty."

"Aye, aye, sir." I dropped to the deck.

The roll call continued by city and state, subjecting seven more Pennsylvanians to close interrogation. But Snake was not satisfied.

"I'm going to look up the next of kin in everyone's record book and I had better not find any of you who have ever *been* in Philadelphia. When I find that person, he will be a sorry sonofabitch. Now, for the last time, who is from Philadelphia?"

Since I was busy doing pushups, he had never asked me directly if I knew anything about mysterious goings on in Philadelphia, so I had never had to lie. Besides, I was from farm country outside Pittsburgh and that was 300 miles from Philly. Baby Sister had prevailed.

It's Party Time!

The Fire Watch woke me and the other members of my squad at 0200. The Section Leader and our squad leader had decided that Private Weezil needed a little inspiration to get with the program and start showing a little loyalty to his fellow turds.

Weezil had screwed up too many times, costing the platoon and the Section Leader extra pushups and other punishments. His biggest sins were that he made other turds look bad and got them into trouble by his brown-nosing.

Like the time during an evening lecture on Marine Corps History when Hoot asked if anyone knew who the first Mameluke Sword was given to. The whole platoon, including Dumbo, knew the answer from studying our Handbooks, but Weezil eagerly raised his hand and bounced around like he had to go to the bathroom.

Although Hoot was used to his brown-nosing bullshit and handled the Suckup's contribution well, Weezil continued to seek Attaboys at the expense of the rest of his buddies.

Weezil also spent more time writing his girlfriend than he spent on cleaning his rifle and polishing his shoes. He constantly failed rifle inspection and got out of step while we were marching.

The last straw, though, came when our platoon Section Leader, the King of the Turds, was Company Runner, a recruit selected each day from the four recruit platoons in the company to be a 'gofer' for the Company office.

"Sir, you have a telephone call," the Company Runner announced to Sgt. Gibson during an evening rifle instruction class.

"You," Weezil muttered accusingly from the anonymity of the seated herd.

Gibson, who hadn't heard, or *chose* not to have heard, the infraction of referring to the drill instructor in the first person, now had no choice. He had to punish the offender even if he was the Section Leader.

"Get down for pushups. Fifty." This wasn't so horrible a punishment as much as the humiliation. The Section Leader had taken a lot of punishment on behalf of the platoon in his role as senior recruit. Now one of his own had sold him out in a half assed attempt to curry favor with the drill instructor.

You don't want to piss off the King of the Turds. The K of T glared at Weezil the whole time he was doing his pushups. I expected that Weezil would get a visit from the Night People at oh dark thirty.

Our squad leader, a chunky black North Carolinian the DIs called the "Big Bopper," lead us stealthily to Weezil's rack. All twelve of us, dressed in skivvies and shower shoe "flip-flops," surrounded Weezil's rack and awaited Bopper's signal.

The Big Bopper draped a blanket over Weezil's sleeping form and held it over his head. He nodded to the rest of us to take turns delivering a few knuckle sandwiches to Weezil's chest, stomach and legs.

"Ohhhh," Weezil screeched, "Ohhhhh! Oh, come on guys!"

Some gave Weezil an extra shot or two, as Weezil was not well liked. Especially by those he had gotten in trouble. When my turn came, I gave him a couple of good shots to his left leg, of which he seemed to have two, when marching. I didn't like him either, but I figured, what the heck, there but for the grace of God, lay I.

The rest of the platoon lay quietly in their racks, although I knew many of them were awake. I knew they were thanking God they weren't the target but some also wishing they could join in. Several snickered; enjoying that Weezil was getting what was coming to him.

After the exercise was over, the Big Bopper motioned us to our racks and handed the blanket to the Fire Watch. Weezil kept his eyes closed and moaned softly, probably atoning for his prior behavior and resolving to try to keep his fellow turds out of trouble in the future.

At reveille, SSgt. Sword noticed Weezil's bruises and strode over, inspecting Weezil's arms and legs.

"What happened to you, turd?"

"Sir, the private tripped over his foot locker!" It was the only acceptable answer.

"Well," intoned Sword, nodding slightly at the Section Leader, "you had better learn to be more careful in the future."

Help, Chesty!

Three weeks had passed since I got off the train in Yemassee. They were three weeks of pure terror. The Marine Corps had discovered the greatest motivator in the world: fear. Not knowing if at any minute that I might have a screaming DI in my face, whether he would accent his "suggestions" with a punch to the gut, or whether I would be singled out for a blanket party kept me on my psychological toes.

I vaguely remembered the sign at the entrance to Parris Island. It simply proclaimed "U. S. Marine Corps Recruit Depot, Parris Island, South Carolina" without the "*Welcome to.*" It could have just as easily proclaimed "The Silly Civilian Shit Stops Here" or "All hope abandon, ye who enter here."

I learned never to be last at anything but also never to be the first; the early worm doesn't fare too well, either. I learned to spread my fingers when doing pushups and keep my palms off the deck. The entire platoon was still baffled by "Darrell Dottle," even by those turds who had taken Spanish in high school.

In the few seconds before sleep overtook me each night, I began to realize that I was probably not going to be shot or have a heart attack doing two thousand pushups. After all, the economical Corps now had an investment in us turds. They had fed us three times a day for twenty-one days; a total cost of at least seven dollars.

We were knocking down seventy-eight dollars a month pay for a private E-1, under six months' service, so they also owed us at least ten more dollars, after subtracting for our cool haircuts and nifty PX items. Not to speak of the cost of electricity in the barracks, drill instructors' salaries, the use of the equipment, and initial uniform issue.

The frugal Corps was not going to throw away all that money if it could help it. But neither would the drill instructors graduate a recruit if they didn't think him able to defend his buddy's back; instead they'd *make* the recruit physically and psychologically *able* to defend his buddy's back.

I think they had already pruned the platoon of the hopeless cases and could now afford only a couple more, at most. The rest they would salvage and mold into Marines. If the borderline turds made it, fine. If they didn't, they didn't want them on their conscience. In the drill instructors' hut there was a sign to remind them:

> "Let's be damn sure
>
> That no man's ghost will
>
> Ever say "IF YOUR
>
> TRAINING PROGRAM
>
> HAD ONLY DONE ITS JOB"

Sgt. Snake, a.k.a. Rasputin, a.k.a. Robespierre, took this motto to heart. His idea of a training program was chock full of sadistic punishments and mocking sarcasm; he was a gifted tormentor. Snake was driven with purpose, and that purpose was to separate the boys from the girls. And after that, the men from the boys.

Snake had one of his many chances one day when Gooney Bird fouled up on the parade ground for what seemed the hundredth time. We were marched "home" in shame, knowing that we were once again headed to the woodshed.

"Get in front of your racks with your weapons," Snake snarled, his agile mind thinking up a new punishment. We stood there at "order arms"; our rifles nestled against our right legs.

"Port, arms," Snake ordered, and we brought our rifle up diagonally across our bodies.

"Hold the weapons straight out in front of you! All the way out! Put your weapons on your knuckles! Give me that!" He ripped the rifle out of the closest turd's hands.

"Hold your hands out! Palms down!" He laid the rifle on the very ends of the turd's fingers, the turd's arms drooping. "Get your arms back up there! Is it too heavy for you, Sweetie?"

We all quickly imitated the move, positioning the rifle on our knuckles.

Snake stomped around the squadbay, pushing up arms, pulling rifles out to the fingertips, and straightening backs.

"Hold them out there! Straighten those arms! Keep those backs straight!"

My nine and a half-pound brother lay like dead weight and the effort soon strained the muscles in my arms and back. Snake went down to the end of the squadbay and squinted along the lines of outstretched rifles.

"Better get that rifle up, Gooney Bird. You're the reason we're all in here!"

But Gooney Bird's rifle was no lower than anyone else's and even higher than those of us on the "Little End." Snake concentrated on the larger turds, holding them to a more exacting standard. Seemed fair to me. If a hundred and fifty pound turd had to hold a *nine* and a half pound rifle, a two hundred pound turd should have a *twelve* and a half pound rifle. Three pounds of rifle for every fifty pounds of turd. Simple proportion.

As the minutes dragged on, the effort was coming unbearable and I lost my interest in math. I struggled to keep up with the rest of the turds. Some of the smaller turds had let their rifles slip down almost to their sides and some were sniffling and sobbing. I grimaced and strained, not daring to drop my brother on his ass on the deck.

There was Snake approaching. Was he looking at me? Was today the day that he'd make an example of me? Scream in my face until I burst into tears and called him a rotten little motherfucker like Randazzo?

He walked in front of me and searched my face. I had learned never to look a DI in the eye, so stared straight ahead at nothing. Disappointed, he walked behind my back, making what little hair I had stand on end. Snake gave me the willies. You never knew when he would unexpectedly grab your Adam's apple from behind or jump in front of your face and deliver a rabbit punch to your gut. I tensed my throat and stomach, just in case.

Maybe today he would make me his special target and start a campaign to get rid of me. And he could do it too, if he wanted to. I was so tired. If I had to hold the rifle for five minutes more I'd probably not be able to. Would he get so disgusted with me that he'd actually punch me or throw me against the wall? Paranoia. Fear.

Finally, I heard his footsteps moving on. Now I had only to deal with the agony of keeping my rifle from slipping out of my grasp and onto the floor.

Dropping your rifle was as unforgivable as telling the DI that he too, was lower than whaleshit and had shit for brains. I knew that from personal experience. Performing rifle drill one day, I lost my grip on my brother as he was traveling from left shoulder arms to port arms. Staring straight ahead, I brought my left hand up to smack my rifle as it came down from my right shoulder. It traveled past my fingertips and clattered on the asphalt. Snake halted the platoon and screamed in my face for a full two minutes. That night I shared my rack with my brother and five of his cousins. That is, I lay on six rifles spread across my rack under my back, waist and legs. I got little, if any, sleep that night.

So I dare not drop the rifle. I grunted and gasped a few more seconds, knowing I was coming to the absolute end of my endurance. This was pain in the first degree. Chesty, help me!

As I blinked and gritted my teeth, the turd across from me came into focus. Private Mainhart, an old guy of twenty-two, was also straining and gasping, tears streaming down his face. He was *crying*! Judas Priest! He was married and even had a kid. Over six feet tall and over two hundred pounds, and he was crying! He was the Section Leader, for God's sake!

Here I was, a turd on the Little End, only five feet eight inches, holding a nine and a half pound rifle, just like his, making faces, moaning and gasping to be sure, but not crying!

The Section Leader was an All-American football player at the University of Virginia. King of the Turds. And I had kept up with him! Damn! Damn! I was doing it! I was keeping up!

My rifle got at least an ounce lighter and I knew I could do this! I would *not* drop my rifle. I would hold out as long as necessary. I knew that I *could* make it through Parris Island.

For the first time, my English teacher's droning of Henley's poem meant something to me.

"Black as the pit from pole to pole,

I thank whatever gods may be

For my unconquerable soul."

And with a little help from Chesty, I would prevail.

For me, it was the moment of truth.

Later I realized that the King of Turds' tears were not of fear, but of frustration. But whatever they were, they helped me through one of my most difficult times in boot camp.

CHAPTER 13 – AND ON WITH THE SHOW

Second Wind

After our hair had a chance to grow an eighth of an inch, we marched a few blocks to the Triangle PX where we had purchased our first PX issue. Here we waited outside for our next haircut. As my turn came I was surprised that I got to set in a chair like I was going to get a real haircut, and maybe chat with the barber about Parris Island gossip, the weather, and how the general was doing. However, again we had no choice in specifying a desired style and the envious bald barber delivered the sheep shearing special. The haircut was delivered in silence and in forty-five seconds.

The highlight of the trip was that the barber had a radio and after the advertisements, the D.J. played "Nel Blu Di Pinto Di Blu," a popular song. It was the first music I'd heard in weeks and reminded me that there was another whole world out there.

Our green utilities began to lose their dark green color and fade a little. Soap stains also helped lighten the fabric.

A few dozen times out on the parade ground earned us our guidon flag with 2037, our platoon number neatly stitched in gold letters. We felt that, at last, we had an identity. Seems like a small thing, but to march behind our little red flag fluttering in the breeze was progress.

We had learned, for the most part, how to begin and stop marching, generally keep in step, turn left and right, and perform much of the rifle manual. Sure, we constantly screwed up, but we were on our way.

Marching with the "Big End" leading.
Photo courtesy of United States Marine Corps.

Sword and Snake were exacting drillmasters and we probably averaged only a foot marched per pushup. One advantage to marching on the Little End was that we were the last to receive extra instruction, a.k.a. punishment.

For example, a "column left" was begun by the leading, or tallest turds. This means only the front part of the column turns to the left while the trailing end of the platoon keeps marching straight until they got to the turning point before also turning left. Turds who couldn't manage to turn to the left in a military manner would get their feet stamped on or kicked out from under them, bodily jerked out of ranks, rabbit punched in the gut, or received other learning tips.

The drill instructors stood in place at the turning point, watching critically as the platoon filed by them by height. So by the time the Little End reached the turning point, we had ample opportunity to learn from the mistakes of the preceding turds on the Big End. Trying to turn left with a drill instructor's foot nailing your shoe to the pavement could give you a hernia. We may have had no leadership potential, but we became fast learners. That was the difference between the quick and the punished.

A disadvantage of marching on the Little End was that when marching off the parade ground, we ate a lot of dust. The turd in front of me also constantly ate too many beans and frequently farted with each step he took. I threatened to light a match and blow his ass up if he didn't lay off the beans.

Marching was a science. You took a thirty-inch step, you swung your arms just so, your rifle was pointed at the sky in the exact same angle as everyone else's, and you "set your heels." Setting your heels meant making a crisp noise when your foot struck the deck. That way the platoon could be heard marching in a crisp "tramp, tramp" and needed no cadence.

There must have been a fine line between "setting your heels" and goose stepping, because I was constantly told not to goose step. I never discovered how to make a heel touching the pavement make a noise without putting some force behind it.

After a few dozen miles and a few days of marching, I developed the condition known as "cracked heels." My heels felt like they had bad toothaches, aching even while I was sitting at chow or while lying in my rack at night. I took to putting pads of toilet paper in my shoes to cushion the pain.

The drill instructors occasionally asked whether there were any recruits with pain in their heels. No way was I going to tell them, however. Cracked heels were a guaranteed way to be sent to sick bay for a couple of weeks, then "set back" to a junior platoon. I would worry about cracked heels after I was at least five hundred miles north of Parris Island.

We were instructed in the Manual of Arms, a precise order in which you moved your brother from one shoulder to the other. We also had an unofficial Manual of Feet.

"Hudgins take a 30-inch step. You're not trying out for the Rockettes."

"Washington, quit ditty bopping."

"Joyce, quit goose stepping! Set your heels!"

The rifle manual movements included moving the rifle from the deck to your right shoulder to port arms to your left shoulder and back a couple of dozen times. Each time you moved your rifle, you smacked the stock to make a distinct, crisp sound. When seventy-five turds smacked their rifle at the same time it sounded very military.

"Right shoulder, harms!" Crack, crack, crack. My brother did not seem to mind this abuse, but it did sting my hands.

A more painful moment sometimes occurred when we performed "inspection arms." This was done when the platoon was halted in formation. The drill instructor would walk along the line, halt, and perform a left face to face a recruit.

The recruit would then bring the rifle up smartly from the deck to port arms, making sure to smack the stock. Arriving at port arms, he pushed the rifle bolt back with his right thumb, glanced down to make sure there was no round in the chamber, then looked up.

You had to be alert because the drill instructor would at any moment lash out and slap the rifle from your grasp. If you let go too soon, the rifle could escape both your grasps and fall to the deck. *Your* fault, of course.

If you hung on too long, and the drill instructor stung his little hands on an immovable rifle, that was *your* fault, too. You never knew when the devious Snake might make a false move for the rifle, and not take it.

When the drill instructor slapped your rifle out of your hands, he spun it over, and in a deft movement, thrust the butt into the air and looked up the barrel. He scrutinized the rifle and all its parts, looking for rust, excess oil, or the dull gleam that said you didn't rub enough linseed oil on the stock. We used one of our three toothbrushes and various rifle tools to scour our brother's hide of rust and other impure substances. We hid the rifle tools in a neat little hole in my brother's butt.

When the DI was satisfied that the rifle was clean, he'd twirl it like a baton, coming to a whirling stop with a smack in front of your face. The recruit was then to take the rifle back like he really wanted it, smacking it out of the drill instructor's hands.

Sometimes the drill instructor was not ready to return the rifle. Since we were to smack the rifle out of his hand, sometimes you smacked an immovable brick and your hand stung for a couple of days.

"I didn't hand you the rifle, *Numb Nuts*! When I extend it to you, you will take it! Did you *intend* to strike me, turd?" Snake, of course.

After retrieving your rifle, you held the bolt back with the knife edge of your right hand, pushed down the follower with your thumb, and let the bolt slam home. With or without a thumb in it.

Sometimes the bolt moved forward like a freight train, grabbing your thumb before you could escape the damn thing. This efficiently punished you for being half awake. The resulting flat piece of bloody flesh was called an "M1-Thumb."

I slapped the shit out of my brother a couple of times for being over zealous for getting his bolt back too quickly. I learned how to eat with my forefinger and index finger while my thumb recuperated.

Letters, He Gets Letters

Private Fanelli got the most letters at every mail call. Most were perfumed and all were in different handwriting. Even the drill instructors noticed.

"Fanelli," SSgt. Sword demanded, "who are all these women who keep writing you?"

"Sir, the private's sisters," Fanelli claimed.

"Bullshit," Sword spat "why do they all have different last names?"

"Sir, the private's sisters are all married!"

Since Fanelli had an adjoining bunk, I asked him later if that were true.

"Sheeet, no," Fanelli confided, "all my sisters are married, but these letters aren't from them! These are from my *special* friends. I figure by the time I get home from boot camp, half of them will have gone off with some other swingin' dick! You gotta have backup!"

I asked him how he got all the girls to write to him and he graciously shared his formula.

"First you gotta tell them that you always had your eye on them and were always too shy to tell them. Then, say you are coming home in a few weeks as a Marine and you'd love squiring them around in your uniform, which the Corps doesn't allow you to take off, even on leave. Make sure they live in different parts of town so they don't get to telling each other about you. Sheeet, man, its easy!"

"What kind of girls do you write to," I asked, impressed.

"All kinds. You need different kinds; girls to go to the show and parking with, girls to bring home to Momma, one or two Rosie Rottencrotches, you *know*!" He winked.

"All you do is write a different one each day and tell them they keep us so busy here you can't write them more than once a week. Then say you have time to read, though, and ask them to write *you* everyday. Some will drop off after a while; that's why you need to have some replacements ready."

He helped me write my first letter, which I decided to send to four girls, changing only the name.

"Dear Norma:

You probably didn't know, but I've been watching you for some time now and finally got up the nerve to tell you. Maybe it's because I'm so far away, training with the Marine Corps at Parris Island, and the distance gives me the courage.

I've always meant to ask you out, but I thought a pretty girl like you would probably be too busy. Anyway, I'd really like to hear from you during the tough training here. Your letters would make a tremendous difference to me and help get through the bad times.

I'll be home in a few short weeks and I daydream about taking you to the show or to church. The Corps is very strict and makes us wear our uniforms all the time. Even while I'm home on leave.

I'm really looking forward to hearing from you, if you're not too busy. Maybe I can even bring you a little present, like a Marine Corps locket, so that you can show your friends that you have a special friend in the Corps.

Fondly,

Turd"

And "Dear Carole" and "Dear Mary" and "Dear Nancy" and "Dear Michelle". I wondered about Henrietta the majorette. And what about Pat the cheerleader? This could be a bonanza! I decided to add them both. And an Antoinette? Ahhhh, Sweet Antoinette!

Get Lost, Buster!

After several weeks we became gourmets of the food at the chow hall. We learned to avoid Sgt. Stagliano's Chicken Parmigiana de Napoli and Sgt. O'Reilly's County Down White Cod. It was easy to be discriminating since the mashed potatoes looked like vanilla milkshakes, grits looked like mashed potatoes and the French fries looked like yellow beans. The yellow beans, of course, looked like French fries. And tasted like them.

Combined with their rigid diets and extra exercise, steering clear of these delicacies helped to trim the fat off the Fat Asses; one of which claimed that he lost so much weight his shoes were now too big.

Even though Duncan Hine's blessings didn't extend to the Ken-L Ration class of restaurants, several turds ate enough to gain weight. "Are you going to eat that," Buffalo Butt frequently whispered when I stared at the remnants of dissected frogs, bats and armadillos. If he didn't quit eating everything on the menu and soon acquire a taste for healthy food, he'd be a candidate for the Fat Man's Platoon.

We knew all the prayers on the grace card by heart and could efficiently rattle off the shortest one, order "ready seats" and be eating in ten seconds. Our prayer probably should have been longer, especially when Stagliano cooked.

No longer did we have to sit at attention, but neither were we allowed to talk, visit, or have food fights.

Sgts. Sword and Gibson generally let us eat in peace while they ate in the partitioned Sergeants' Mess, but Snake continued to harass us. Sonofabitch was never hungry. He would jump in front of our faces while we were busily eating and point out some infraction on etiquette.

"Close your mouth when you chew, Dumbo! You sound like a cow chewing cud. Or are you stomping grapes? Just gulp your food, Goony Bird! Did your dog teach you to eat? Thompson, sit up straight." I wondered if the Corps' answer to Emily Post was also going to tell us to eat our peas because people in India were starving. Maybe we could send them some SOS.

The chow never improved, but sometimes they tried to make up for it with variety. Like the time they had Mexican, boiled taco, I think. That was a treat.

Another time they tried Chinese. Scorched sweet and sour turkey. One time they even had fortune cookies. Other than the *Guidebook for Marines*, it was the only piece of reading material I had seen in weeks. I was eager to see if Confucius had an encouraging word for me. I broke it apart and quickly read my fortune.

"You will meet a tall, dark-haired beauty. She will have lots of money and drive a mint green T-Bird." Wow! I turned the fortune paper over to read the rest.

"She will not like you."

Well, it started off well. She wouldn't like Snake, Sword, Gibson, O'Reilly or Stagliano, either.

I had learned to eat the meat and the dessert first in case the DI unexpectedly stood up and left. You didn't want to be the last one out so you ate like someone was going to steal your food. If you were a nibbler rather than a gulper, you just might run five miles around the platoon as it marched to its next destination.

I thought heavy exercise after eating was bad for the digestion. You could get cramps. Snake would probably take us swimming if that were the case.

Neither Sgts. O'Reilly nor Stagliano ever met us at the door on the way out to ask if everything was all right. That was okay; we never left a tip, either.

CHAPTER 14 – DOOM AND GLOOM

Showdown at the Triangle PX

An ill-timed chuckle while standing in front of the Triangle PX gave the omnipresent 3-striped reptile a chance to nail me again for frivolous behavior.

"Private Joyce will entertain the customers with squat thrusts," Snake announced to the platoon, "while the rest of you ladies will enter the PX and make your purchases."

There, on the walkway of the entrance of the PX, I dropped to my haunches, put my hands on the deck, snapped my legs back under me, retrieved my legs, and then stood up. Many times.

This was one of my most hated pastimes because it quickly made my legs feel like rubber. It was done by the numbers, like everything else. One, dipping down, two, extending your legs behind you, three, contracting your legs, and four, returning to standing position.

After I had ran off a dozen or so, Snake went into the PX, probably to ensure that none of the shitheads bought any personality changing laxatives or other controlled substances. Who knew what a laxative would do to a turd? He might explode. Thunderturd.

"*Thirty-eight*, two, three, four! *Thirty-nine*, two, three, four!"

This was really getting old. My thighs burned and my lungs fought for air. My cracked heels became more and more painful. I imagined myself the perpetual turd, never to graduate. I worried about my cracked heels. Could you get cracked heels from hoping you didn't get them?

Entering and departing customers, both Marines and

civilians passed by, amused and grinning. Okay for *you* to chuckle and smile, I thought viciously. You take slouching as a right, not a privilege that must be earned. Silly civilian shits.

One little nipper, about four or five years old, dropped down beside me and tried to imitate me doing the squat thrusts. His mother, with her Dependent's Card already out for the PX cashier, was probably a Marine's wife.

"What's he doing, Mommy," he asked, peering into my sweating face.

"He's doing his exercises, Honey," she informed the little guy, "he has to do them to be big and strong."

Exercises, my star-spangled ass, lady, I thought bitterly. This was agony!

"*Fifty-eight*, two, three, four!"

Man, this was *torture*! Help! My legs are killing me! My breath came in ragged gasps. That was why we called squat thrusts "Huff 'n Puffs."

Where in the hell was Snake? Still inside, probably laughing it up with the salesgirl or promoting rifle oil sales.

"*Sixty-five*, two, three, four!"

In the PX's glass front door I saw the reflection of a Marine approaching from behind. I could see the silver bars of a first lieutenant on his shirt collar wings.

"*Ninety-six*, two, three, four," I moaned, jumping the tally thirty counts.

The lieutenant stopped in front of me and waited until I completed the count and returned to my feet.

"Stop there, Private," he ordered, "where's your drill instructor?"

"Sir, the private's," I stopped to catch much-needed

breath, pitifully, I hoped, "drill instructor is in the PX!"

"Wait here," the splendid lieutenant ordered and entered the PX.

I wondered if I should resume my squat thrusts. The lieutenant didn't say stop doing them altogether and feel free to lounge around; he just said "wait here." But if Snake came back out alone, I couldn't very well say some wonderful officer had commanded me to stop. On the other hand, if the lieutenant came out with him, he might ask why I had ignored his order to stop.

A sergeant is only four rungs up from me on the food chain, while the lieutenant was *ten* rungs up. I decided to go with the lieutenant.

I stood, mostly at attention, and saluted a Captain on his way out of the PX and smiled at some laughing teenage girls on their way in. I was a kind of unofficial greeter.

After a few minutes, the lieutenant and Snake appeared and I resumed the position of silent sentinel at attention. The lieutenant motioned Snake aside and spoke to him in low tones. From the way Snake nodded respectfully, I didn't take it that the lieutenant was congratulating him on my record number of squat thrusts.

As the lieutenant continued on his way into the PX, Snake approached and glared at me. After a long scathing scowl, he told me to "get inside."

I wobbled into the PX and thanked God that Snake didn't have the necessary mental gymnastics to estimate squat thrusts per minute. I noticed that cigars were still not on the list.

Requiem for a Downed Flyer

Besides the drill instructors, one of our other tormentors was the sand fleas. These little varmints could bite like a good-sized dog if they could get into your ear, nose, or the corner of your eye. You could hear them coming; the buzzing increased in pitch like a small motorbike going 90 miles an hour, then you felt a pinch as sharp as a needle.

Snake enlisted the sand fleas and seemed to command squadrons of them. He frequently took us to a sand pit where the fleas had their base camp and were on 24-hour alert. There he had us stand in formation with our hands in our pockets, while his friends dined on us at will. We served them according to their appetite; light snack, dinner, or the Red Cross Donation.

One day, as Sgt. Snake was giving us the usual lecture on the atrocious progress we were making on our marching, I heard an approaching flight of flying teeth. One of the greedy kamikazes peeled of and alighted on my cheek.

After scouting around awhile surveying prime flesh, he staked his claim, and started to draw blood. I felt the needle dipping in once, twice, three times. The little shit was half vampire and I grew tired of getting stuck for his dinner.

Snake seemed preoccupied by another turd at the front of the formation, so I dispatched the gluttonous bug with a quick swipe.

"Joyce! Get your ass up here!" Snake came whistling around the platoon. No surprise. Sonofabitch could see around corners.

"I saw that! You *killed* that sand flea! You *murdered* him," he screamed. "That flea probably had kids! You fuckin' orphaned them, you heartless shit!"

I tried to look as contrite as I could, within the stone face requirements of attention, of course.

"He's gotta eat too," Snake raved on, circling me. "He didn't eat that much!"

Hell he didn't. The miserable little shit must have been stocking up for the winter.

"You recover his body! Right now!"

I stood there dumbfounded. How was I going to find a body the size of a pencil point?

"His ass is still on your check, Numb One!" He pointed at my face. "Reach up and get it!"

Reaching up, I felt the little maggot and retrieved his remains.

"Was it a male or a female, Killer," he asked.

Shit, how the hell would I know? Was there a bounty on males?

"Sir, it was a *male*," I suggested.

"How the hell would *you* know, turd?"

"Sir, the private would never hit a female!"

"Ohh, you're a wiseass, are you, Joyce?"

"No, Sir!" Actually, I probably was, but sometimes I heard what I said along with everyone else.

"Get down there," he pointed to a patch of dirt, "and dig me a one foot square hole with your bayonet!"

I laboriously carved up a grave for the deceased while his next of kin and mourners dined on my neck, ears, and fellow turds.

"Lay his ass in there! Gently!" Snake was really into this.

"Well, say a few words for him, Killer!" Snake waited, expectantly.

My mind went blank. Oh Great Bug in the Sky, receive our dearly departed...

"Are you a goddamned heathen? Haven't you ever

been to a funeral?" Snake reached over and grabbed my Adam's apple. "You better think of something, turd!"

"Ashes to ashes and dust to dust. Amen," I croaked, respectfully.

"Well, that didn't give *me* no fuckin' comfort, turd, but maybe these goddammed bugs don't know the difference. Cover it up. *Gently*!"

I solemnly scraped the dirt into the hole and jumped to my feet.

"You're at *attention*! This is a *funeral*, you ignorant shits! Hand, *salute*! Ready, *two*!"

"Make him a cross," Snake ordered. "and write out his inscription in the dirt: 'Here lies A. Sandflea, murdered by a heartless turd. R.I.P.'"

I twisted a couple of weeds together in a makeshift cross, pushed it into the ground, and scratched out the incriminating epitaph in the dirt with my bayonet.

Satisfied that the recently downed miniature wing wiper had received his full burial honors, Snake stomped to the front of the platoon.

I "inadvertently" stomped on the departed's grave as I resumed my place in the platoon.

"Don't *ever* let me see any of you kill another of God's creatures! They gotta eat too! It's about the only thing you turds are good for!"

And funeral services were over.

Reservation for Cpl. Winston

Mess duty was not fun. On the first day we had to get up at 0330, otherwise known as "oh dark thirty." We marched to the mess hall by 0400 and were finished only when we cleaned up after the last chow for the day. We didn't get back to our barracks until an hour or two before taps.

We wore white trousers and shirts and white paper overseas caps, or "piss cutters." We looked like little Dutch Boys on our way to plugging a dike or painting a house.

The only good thing about it was that we hardly saw the drill instructors, except for marching us to and from the mess hall. No marching, no PT, no pushups, no sand flea funerals. Once in a while they'd come to check on us, maybe to hear the dirt from the two mess sergeants, O'Reilly and Stagliano.

O'Reilly was a walrus of a man; his overhanging belly confirming that he constantly sampled his cooking. Stagliano was tall and lean, obviously not much of a cook.

Each had his specialties, O'Reilly with his County Cork Style Green Beans and Famous Belfast Beans. Stagliano's Naples Style Green Beans and Fancy Firenza Beans tasted suspiciously like County Cork Green Beans and Famous Belfast Beans, however.

We had all sorts of exotic dishes and associated names to identify them. Hamburgers were "sliders," hot dogs were "rollers," baloney was "tube steak," smaller baloney was "horse cock," and small breakfast sausages were "monkey dicks." Chicken a la King was "dynamited chicken," and of course, creamed chipped beef on toast was the famous "shit on a shingle," or SOS. Pot roast was sometimes known as "boiled rat," and fried fish on toast was known as "lizard sandwich."

I hung around Sgt. Stagliano one morning in the crematory, or kitchen, watching to see how he prepared the daily ration of SOS. Partly to see if there was any basis for some of the turds referring to it as "creamed foreskins." He proudly advised that it was a staple of the Corps and had to be processed in a steam vat almost like cereal. I left before he assured me it was the breakfast treat shot from guns.

After attending chow for weeks without any dessert;

cake, cookies, pie, candy, I craved chocolate and sweets. My biggest treat came when I brushed my teeth with Ipana *spearmint* toothpaste. I liked any dessert except gelatin. Red jello, yellow jello, orange jello. My least favorite was green jello. Once on Thanksgiving we had a piece of pumpkin pie but no coffee was ever served. Only orange juice, milk, and koolade, or "bug juice." Bug juice was a colored sweetened drink that tasted the same no matter what color it was. Even so, my favorite color was red. The DIs said we had to have 5000 calories a day to make fighting machines out of us but that chocolate and coffee would deteriorate our body temples.

My main job was "pots and pans man," but I also got nabbed for swabbing the decks, peeling potatoes, taking out the garbage cans, and filling salt and peppershakers.

Scrubbing pots and pans was a chore until I used some of the tricks I had learned from my part time job as a dishwasher in high school.

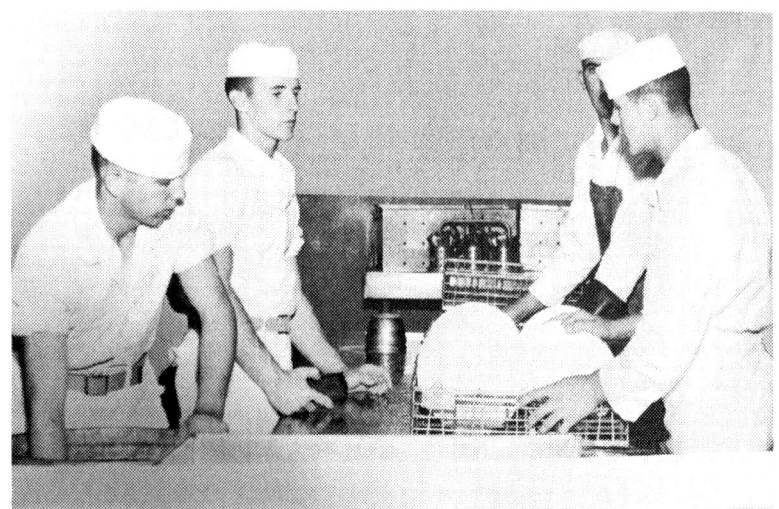

Mess men in their nifty outfits.
Photo courtesy of United States Marines Corps.

I ran half of the pots and pans through Buffalo Butt's dish and silverware scullery when the mess sergeants weren't looking. The other half I submerged in the giant steam heated cooking vats until the cooking materials boiled off. Then I simply opened the heated ovens and laid them on the open doors to dry.

I carefully inspected the salt shakers and salt supply for the infamous saltpeter. Seeing nothing suspicious, I wondered if they could disguise it as "pepperpeter." Pepperpeter sounded like a problem and a benefit at the same time.

Taking the garbage out was my favorite job as I could sneak a smoke and visit with Corporal Winston. Winston showed up everyday without fail after noon and evening chow. Since Stagliano usually cooked morning chow with his SOS and horse cock, I couldn't blame Winston for missing that.

Winston's favorites were tube steak and bones. According to Sgt. O'Reilly, we were to set aside any leftovers in this category for the good Corporal, which meant fishing in the garbage cans.

Weezil and I dragged out the garbage cans one day after evening chow and fished through the leftovers. Weezil, although much reformed from his blanket party, didn't care much for dogs and made only a cursory search for Winston's treats. Winston, eyeing the sparse bounty ending up on his dish, growled and looked up at Weezil.

"There's nothing in there, Slobbers, you're SOL today." Weezil told Winston, and fished a cigarette out of his pack.

Winston again looked at his dish, then turned back to Weezil, growling loudly.

"You better find him a bone or something," I warned Weezil.

As to confirm that Weezil better find *something*, Winston started barking, steadily eyeing Weezil.

"Hell, he's just a dumb dog," Weezil said, lighting his cigarette, "he'll just leave in a minute. The fat ass could stand to miss a meal."

At which Corporal Winston launched forward and grabbed Weezil by the leg, growling furiously.

"Okay, okay," Weezil screamed.

"I think its 'okay, *sir*,'" I offered.

"Okay, *sir*!"

Winston stopped growling, but hung onto Weezil's leg.

Weezil stretched over to the garbage can and withdrew a bone.

"Here, sir," he offered, "I found one. See, it's a bone, sir!"

Winston let go of Weezil's leg but stood there glaring at him for a few moments, then burst into another barking fit. Weezil and I stood there helplessly, not knowing what to do.

The door behind us banged open and Sgt. O'Reilly stood, hands on hips, in the doorway.

"What the hell's going on out here," O'Reilly demanded.

Winston turned to him and started yapping.

"You turds trying to short Corporal Winston out of his chow? You people are fucking with an NCO! Maybe you'd like to stay tonight and serve midnight chow for the Guard Relief? You fuck with Corporal Winston, you fuck with *me*!"

To accent the warning, Winston lumbered over to Weezil, lifted his leg and pissed on Weezil's ankle. That done, he inspected his dish and selected a bone to gnaw.

"You okay with that, Corporal Winston?"

Winston yapped his grudging approval and took off at a trot with his bone, probably to see if the pickings were any better at the First Battalion mess hall.

For the rest of my mess duty, I made sure Corporal Winston got his share of bones and tube steak. He usually grunted his thanks but didn't water or chew on my leg.

Telephone Pole, Anyone?

An integral part of every day was filled with physical training, or "PT." Both unofficial and official. The unofficial kind occurred at any hour of the day or night at the whim of a disappointed drill instructor.

The official kind was led every morning by our instructor Chuck. A couple of weeks into the program, Chuck had taken to showing off by clapping his hands while doing his pushups. Later he graduated to doing them one-handed.

"A while back you learned how to stop doing pushups like women," he advised. "You can do a few of them now, but now you do them like boys. Today, you're going to learn how to do them like *men*. Assume the position!"

We got down and held ourselves off the ground, ready to obtain our manhood.

"You will start at the top position and lower yourself as normal. When you get to the bottom, push yourself strongly off the ground. You need to get some height so you can clap in time to get your hands under you again. Otherwise, gravity will win and you will hug the dirt. Okay, let's try a few. Clapping pushups, *begin*!"

The platoon made a collective grunt as gravity won by a large margin. Most of us found it very hard to clap after our stomachs had already hit the ground.

"That's okay," Chuck consoled, "we'll work on it. Soon we'll be doing five, then ten or more. The more we work, the more energy you'll have."

"Later, we'll learn how to do one-handed pushups. They're easy once you get used to them." He dropped down with one arm behind his back and grandstanded ten quick one-handed pushups.

"You *do* want to learn how to do them, don't you?"

Hell yes, Chuck; it's been a lifelong dream. What's next, leaping tall buildings?

To keep us from leaving the PT field with any recognizable trace of energy, Chuck had designed a piece of "exercise equipment." This was simply a metal telephone pole, wrapped in a sleeve of canvas.

How this complex piece of equipment worked was that eight turds picked up the pole and then lay down, with the pole on our chests. Sit-ups are more exciting with a log threatening to march across your Adam's apple.

Why are these guys smiling?
Photo courtesy of United States Marine Corps.

Somehow they turned carrying your buddy into a race. Photo courtesy of United States Marine Corps.

To limber up after lumberjack sit-ups, we ran a few laps around the field with the pole raised over our heads. You'd have thought that a person of normal intelligence would have rested the pole on our shoulders, but maybe we were trying to air it out after contact with our sweating T-shirts.

As a special treat, Chuck occasionally declared what he called a "field meet." Our competitors were turds of our sister platoon 2038, the noisy turds who resided in the topside squad room in our barracks.

One of the events in the Turd Olympics was draping a fellow turd over your shoulder and running a hundred yards and back. A variation was cradling him like a baby and running the same course. With turds from our sister platoon running against us, we were made to think this was a race. The winners got nothing. The losers earned extra "instruction."

Another event was apparently scheduled only for rainy days, in which the field turned into a giant puddle. The piece of equipment used was an eight-foot inflatable canvas ball. The idea was to get the ball from your side of the field to the opposite side. That was the entire set of rules. The ball was so heavy that kicking it only dislocated your ankle. Throwing cross body blocks against the ball would sometimes make it quiver. Only the combined force of at least ten or fifteen turds strenuously pushing got the thing to roll at all.

Once it got up a head of steam, it took tremendous force to stop. Turds on the opposite side got flattened trying to stop it with only five or so bodies. Practically everyone was spread-eagled in the slop at one time or another, punctuated by footprints across their back.

Occasionally two great forces met and the ball squirted straight up, leaving a few dozen turds pushing at nothing but air, resulting in multiple five-point landings in the slop.

This may have been called "bodyball."
Photo courtesy of United States Marine Corps.

The only recognizable event was the tug of war. This generally ended in a stalemate, as both sides were afraid to lose.

Somehow during these games, somebody kept score between the Christians and the Lions, because the defeated team always incurred the wrath of the shamed drill instructor. A shamed drill instructor leads to punished turds.

The competition between our platoon and our sister platoon 2038 was always intense. Sgt. Frog took every opportunity to needle Snake. From the Initial Strength Test to the Swimming Test to Field Meets, Frog and Snake tried to outdo each other, comparing stats of the number of failing or losing turds in each platoon after every event.

Duck walking off the premises was one of the most

hated punishments. Squatting down on our haunches, we grabbed both ankles and waddled forward either fifty or a hundred yards, depending upon how bad we lost. To keep in step during this key military exercise, we quacked along on our own cadence. Quacking was more understandable than darrell dottling.

If we won, however, we were double-timed back to the barracks singing marching songs. Strains of "I've got a girl that lives on a hill, honey, honey" were popular, but my favorite was "Sweet Antoinette."

Hoot would give us the words and we would shout out the song.

"Sweet Antoinette," he cued.

"Sahweeet Annnntonette," we boomed.

"Your pants are wet."

"Your pannnts are wettttt!"

"You say its sweat."

"You saaayyy it's sweattt!"

"It's piss, I'll bet."

"It's piss, I'll betttt!"

"In all my dreams."

"Innnnn alllll my dreaaaammmmms!"

"Your bare ass gleams."

"Yourrrrr bare ass gllllleaaaammmms!"

"You are the wrecker."

"You are – the wreck kerrrrr!"

"Of my pecker."

"Oooofffffff myyyy peeckkk ekkkkerrrrr!"

"Sweet Antoinette."

"Swwweeeeeetttttt Annnntonnnnettttte!"

"I'll get you yet."

"I'lll get you yyeetttttttt!"

CHAPTER 15 – RIFLE RANGE

Cheek to Cheek

It was still dark when we got our gear together to head for the short trip to the rifle range. Because we had so much to do, the fire watch woke us at oh dark thirty. The only other people up and about at this godforsaken hour were the devil and bad women.

We leapt aboard our luxury travel accommodations, a gray 1948 Chevy bus probably previously used for ten years as a tour cruiser in Guatemala, and traveled about a mile and a half through the flora and fauna on the island to the range.

We disembarked the Good Ship Lollipop and were assigned quarters in Quonset huts; little half moon metal sheds with plywood ends and concrete floors. This was definitely a step down from our former accommodations at the barracks.

Spartan as they were, the Second Battalion World War II frame buildings were at least warm and comfortable. As mentioned, since the Second Battalion area resembled an old western town, we referred to it as "Dodge City." The Third Battalion area, with its enviable brick barracks, was known as "Disneyland." That definitely made the rifle range the "Outback."

It was a busy day. We attended class after class, learning about weapon safety, types of ranges and targets, the four firing positions, how to use the rifle sling to stabilize firing positions, cleaning rifles after firing, and so on.

We were issued the Marine Corps' idea of a shooting jacket, a baggy collarless shirt with a one-eight inch thick "pad" on the shoulder. I supposed the extra one eight inch of cloth was intended for decoration rather than any noticeable cushion against rifle recoil.

On the last trip to the PX, a new item called "blousing garters" were on the list. These were green elastic bands that folded the bottoms of our trousers, trousers because women wear pants, over our high top boots. These made us look like storm troopers and very salty. Bloused trousers showed we had "time in." Very salty.

The rifle range armorer installed another rear sight aperture on my best friend, cautioning me that I would be paying for the next one.

Our first rifle coach, a tobacco chewing gunnery sergeant named Sack, instructed us in the four firing positions. The standing, or offhand, position was first.

"Set your feet at a comfortable distance apart," Gunny Sack instructed, "insuring perfect balance!"

I hadn't been *comfortable* since I got to Parris Island. How was I supposed to remember how to do that? Perfect balance? He must not be talking to us turds. We couldn't do anything good, or even half-assed, let alone achieve perfection in balance. Well, might as well play along, but he was probably used to being disappointed.

"Next, place the rifle in your shoulder and hold it with your left arm when the rifle is in the most comfortable position!"

There he goes again. The most *comfortable*. Why the hell didn't he just say the least painful and be done with it?

"Okay, now grip the small of the stock, holding your right elbow in line with *or* above the shoulder!"

Well, make up your mind, Gunny, which is it? In line *with*, or *above*, the shoulder? The drill instructors never gave us choices. Now they want us to help the rifle coach decide how to do it. We thought *he* knew.

I watched the turds that weren't getting chewed out or having their elbows dislocated by the drill instructors. It looked like the "above the shoulder" choice was winning the poll, so I raised my elbow.

How was I going to remember all this comfortable, perfect balance, and optional elbow shit when the screaming hordes from hell were racing toward my position shooting live bullets? Why didn't we just stand behind a tree and shoot back? Standing out in the open like the Redcoats at Concord seemed to me to be inviting a few hundred machine gun shells in your direction.

The rifle had a mind of its own, weaving and bobbing all around the target, a little black circle painted on a stick in the ground.

The sitting position was easier, especially if you happened to be double jointed.

"For the next position, drop to the ground, breaking your fall with your right hand, but keep your feet in place!"

Only a nitwit would lean back and bounce his ass off the ground without putting his hand out. This stuff was really technical.

"Ouch," one of our nitwits muttered, "why in the hell can't we just sit down?" Turds were beginning to mutter a little as they began to get salty.

"Now place your feet at 45-degree angles and well apart! Hold those ankles straight! Put your left elbow as far as you can down the inside of your left leg!"

Now it *did* get technical.

"Put the butt of the rifle into your shoulder and press your cheek to the stock!"

Almost sort of cheek-to-cheek.

"Now put your right elbow on the inside of your right leg with your hand gripping the small of the stock! The back should be bent well forward!"

The Gunny and the drill instructors circulated through the contorting turds, adjusting elbows and ankles. I huffed as I felt a shoe on my back, driving my chest forward almost into the ground. The helpful Sgt. Snake had just helped another in the ranks to become double jointed. My rifle was now pointed straight at the ground.

"If we ever get attacked by gophers, clown," he observed, "we'll know who to put in the front line."

I tried to rearrange my cheeks and elbows as he went to deliver his expertise to another recruit.

"The third position is the kneeling position." Gunny Sack continued, "drop to one knee, right leg parallel to the target. Left foot at right angles to the right leg midway between foot and knee!"

Shit! By the time I got into this position, the thundering herd would have trampled me and been long gone before I could fire a shot!

"Sit back on your heel. Hold your foot upright!"

This hurt! My shoelaces were now almost flat on the ground! Crunch! My foot didn't hurt anymore as the sonofabitch immediately went numb. And my shoelaces were now flat *on* the ground. The ever-helpful Sgt. Snake strikes again. When they meant flat, they meant a straight line from your toes to your knee to the horizon.

"That's it, Sweetie," he praised happily. The first word of demented approval I could remember since I laid eyes on him.

I wondered if General Hauling or Chesty had any problems getting into the kneeling position. *Every* Marine, private or general, had to qualify each year with US Rifle, Caliber .30, M1. Knowing that both the general and Chesty had to gut out the same contortions I was doing made me feel a little better.

The prone and last position was easy. You just laid on the ground, spread your legs and put your elbow under the rifle. It was also my favorite position, because it was the only time I could lie down before taps. Very restful. I hoped we fired a lot of shots from the prone position.

As I lay in the sand, I spotted dozens of sand fleas, also snapping in for later attacks on ears, cheeks and eyes. I carefully killed off as many of the little bastards as I could, both male *and* female, with little or no remorse.

We were now ready to "snap-in," or dry fire, the weapon. We practiced the standing, sitting, and kneeling positions constantly because the most shots were fired from them. Only ten rounds were fired from prone. No rest for the wicked, or the downtrodden, for that matter.

Hour after hour, day after day; we sat, kneeled, and stood, shooting imaginary bullets at the little black bulls eyes on the sticks. Once in a while, we got to lie on the grass.

Breathe, aim, hold, squeeze. Breathe, aim, hold, squeeze.

I got to know U.S. Rifle, Caliber .30, M1 intimately. Feeling his comfortable butt in my shoulder was beginning to feel like second nature. We were beginning to bond. Lining up the sights on the targets, breathing, aiming, holding, squeezing.

The Sport of Turds

There comes a day, generally after several weeks of training, that a recruit begins to feel "salty." The progression from being "scared shitless" to being "just plain scared" to "deeply respectful" also accompanies the labels "turd," "maggot," "puke," "numb nuts," "pimple on a Marine's ass" to "clown."

In your advancement to "deeply respectful," you

begin to acquire some premature bad habits, such as thinking for yourself, confidence, and pride. Too much of this kind of warrior behavior while you're still a recruit is called "salty."

Anyway, I had reached the lofty plateau of slightly salty clown when the Godfather got the chop.

Cockroaches, or palmetto bugs as they are sometimes known, bunked with us in the Quonset huts. We found that when we squashed them, their bodies left telltale signs of their demise on the floor, so we took to catching them and throwing them outside. Near the DI's hut of course. But we also found they were as fast as speeding bullets.

Dumbo, being a gaming soul from horse racing country in Kentucky, came up with the idea. Some roaches were faster than others and with proper training and an enclosed racecourse, could be used in a sporting game of chance.

After six weeks of training, the DIs discovered Parris Island had a laundry and sent out our utilities. At our expense, of course. The utilities came back starched with cardboard in the shirts. This left more time for marching.

We took two discarded cardboard inserts and constructed a miniature racetrack with lane strips cut with our bayonets. We taped the cardboard strips in two lanes and even adjusted the inside starting position a couple of inches behind the outside lane to even the distance to run.

To entice the speedsters to run, we soaked cotton balls with water and squeezed a couple of drops on unwilling contestants. Since the lane strips were fashioned into an A-shape, the contestants could not easily escape from their assigned lane. An enclosed "hut" at the end of the run permitted the roach to find darkness and temporary security and additionally acted as an incentive to traverse the racecourse.

Amazingly, most of the roaches cooperated, although we had to tap them with a cardboard starter strip from time to time to get the little shitheads' attention.

After a few tryouts, Buffalo Butt Jr., Tinkerbelle, Wonder Woman, and the Godfather were retained in the racing stable. We didn't distinguish between male and female as there seemed to be no apparent weakness on the females' part, whichever they were.

We spent a few days pursuing the Sport of Turds until, at the height of a bitterly contested race between Buffalo Butt Jr. and Wonder Woman, a cinder block crashed through the plywood panel of our Quonset hut's front door.

"Get outside," Snake screamed. "Get outside! Are you goddammed people deaf? 2037 outside!"

We hastily threw the racetrack with its still competing occupants into the GI can, scrambled out to the street and lined up.

"What the hell's going on in there? When I say get outside, I mean get outside on the *goddammed double*!"

Sgt. Snake was beside himself, darting in and out of the formation, pausing to scream in the faces of several clowns.

He stopped in front of Dumbo, the owner of the star cockroach called the "Godfather." Dumbo didn't trust his runner to the normal racing stable quarters, which consisted of an inverted shaving cream can cover. Instead, he separated a finger length of starch in his utility jacket pocket and thrust the "Godfather" in there while he wasn't racing.

Unfortunately for Dumbo, the Godfather was doing his calisthenics inside the shirt pocket to keep limber for the next race. Snake spotted the minute vibrations on the shirt pocket.

"What the hell's in your shirt, Dumbo," Snake demanded, "is that your little heart pounding? What the hell's in there?"

"Sir ..." Dumbo floundered.

"Get whatever the hell's in there out! *Now*, Dumbo!"

Dumbo carefully extracted the Godfather out of his pocket and held him between his thumb and forefinger, Godfather's legs flailing.

"Eat it," Snake screamed.

Immediately Dumbo slapped his mouth with the prize winning Godfather and swallowed.

"Jesus Christ! Jesus Christ," Snake blustered. "You goddammed savage!"

Snake was incredulous. "Go get a drink of water!" He shoved Dumbo toward the water faucet on the side of the Quonset.

Snake was obviously shaken, probably not expecting Dumbo's instant response.

"In the Pacific, Marines ate bugs, worms and snakes," he lectured, regaining his composure, "there may come a day when that's all you can find to eat and you'll be damn glad to find that."

Dumbo returned from the side of the Quonset hut and stood at attention. His normally placid face was placid as usual. Snake shook his head, but looked somewhat more relieved.

We shut down racing operations that afternoon, liberating our speedsters to pursue other career interests. Near Snake's hut, of course.

Winning Our Sandspurs

To celebrate the discovery of the Godfather and the suspicious circumstances surrounding his appearance, Sgt. Snake arranged for us to take a little field trip after evening chow.

It promised to be a leisurely walk in the boondocks, as we had not been told to bring along our brother and best friend, U.S. Rifle, Caliber .30, M1.

We marched through a couple of fields and clumps of trees, arriving at a sandy open stretch.

Then, without any warning, Snake halted the platoon.

"Hit the dirt," he ordered.

We hit the dirt, expecting to hear machine gun fire or approaching airplanes. As I landed on the sand, I felt several excruciating stabbing points prick the palms of my hands, my stomach, and my legs. Looking straight ahead at eye level, I saw the source of my torment - sandspurs. These were little round seeds with needle sharp spikes. They stuck like glue to whatever they touched and hurt like hell.

From the grunts and ouches, I could tell that the crafty Snake had put the entire platoon in a patch of them. Another of his creative punishments.

"All, right! On your feet! Five steps forward, harch! One, two, three, four, five! *Hit the dirt!*"

Ouch! Rotten little bastard must have missed a good patch. The palms of my hands, as well as my knees, had gained some new riders.

"On your backs! Come on, roll over! On your knees! On your feet! Hit the dirt!" Snake was really enjoying this. Next he'd have us take our shoes off, followed by our trousers.

"Are we having fun, turds? Any more roaches belly dancing in our pockets? Let's give them a chance, crawl forward! On your bellies! Get those guts on the ground!"

I crawled forward like a guilty dog, amassing at least thirty or forty sand spurs on one part of my body or another. I felt like a human pincushion.

After soaking up most of the vegetation in the area,

Snake let us stand. We were then marched back to our Quonset huts and stood at attention.

"You people are filthy! Dirty! Skuzzy!"

He moved to Private Dumbo, peering at a sand spur on Dumbo's shirt pocket.

"You got a passenger in there, Dumbo?"

"No, sir," Dumbo yelled truthfully.

"Well, let's be sure," Snake grabbed Dumbo's hand and placed it over the sandspur.

Smack! Snake slapped Dumbo's hand onto the sandspur. He was always using someone else's hand for contact sports.

"Nope," observed Snake, "nothing in *there*."

"Okay, you people look like shit. Get those damn plant seeds off your utilities. Get your buddies to get them off your back and ass. Just pretend you're monkeys picking lice."

Dance, Buckaroo

We snapped in for all three weeks we were at the rifle range. Even on the third week, when we actually fired live ammunition, we still snapped in.

Finally, after two weeks, came the day when we were marched up to the firing line at 200 yards to fire our first shot. We were again subjected to a marathon lecture about safety on the range in which we were never to point a loaded rifle anywhere but the target.

The first firing position was the offhand, or standing, position. I cinched my rifle strap, spread my feet, put my elbow under the stock, and clicked on the safety.

"With a clip of eight rounds, lock and load," the

range officer announced over a PA system. He nervously looked up and down the line of twenty five armed turds.

We pulled the bolt back, depressed the follower, and inserted the eight-round clip, letting the bolt fly forward. All twenty five turds successfully completed the maneuver without catching any thumbs in the bolt.

Somewhat reassured, he continued. "Ready on the left, ready on the right! Ready on the firing line! Unlock!"

I released the safety, awaiting the order to fire.

"You may commence firing when ready! Fire on your own target!"

My rifle coach raised my right elbow a little higher, pushed my left elbow a little further under my weapon, and told me to breathe, aim, hold, and squeeze.

Blam! My best friend, my brother, U.S. Rifle, Caliber .30, M1, kicked me hard in the shoulder, probably for the time I dropped him in the squadbay. The target went down and I waited for the result.

The target stayed down. Had I missed? How could I have missed the whole damned target? Maybe I had shot on Buffalo's target. God knows, he needed the extra shot.

Finally, the target came up and my coach grabbed his binoculars.

"Put on three clicks of elevation and two clicks of right windage!"

I adjusted the sights and tried another shot.

"One more click of elevation. Hold it steady."

I fired another shot. And another.

"Okay, you got a nice group. Log this 'dope' in your scorebook: At 200 yards, four clicks elevation, two clicks of right windage."

I fired off my ten rounds, then went to sit on a bench

to let the second third of the platoon shoot ten rounds for their dope. There were fifty targets and two platoons were firing in groups of twenty-five turds each.

As I watched our rival platoon, 2038, I noticed that everywhere Sgt. Frog went, so did two tall recruits with rifles. He was afraid some turd was going to take a shot at him and had two bodyguards! From my brief acquaintance with him at Receiving, I could see how he might be concerned about having to outrun a nasty metal wasp, chasing him at 2160 feet per second, the muzzle velocity of US Rifle Caliber .30, M1.

I looked back at our turds, firing in the second wave. The bandy-legged Sgt. Snake rushed back and forth, harrying the shooters, and generally passing out his usual ration of shit. I wondered if I disliked or hated him enough to take a shot at him.

No, not really, I thought. Maybe just pepper the ground at his feet with a full clip. Make him dance like a cowboy. "Dance, Buckaroo, *dance!*" I thought of him tap dancing and shuffling his legs like the Blue Mountain Cloggers and felt better for it.

We moved back to the 300-yard line.

Buffalo in the Butts

Once a day on the last week it was our turn to "pull the butts." The platoon was marched to a concrete trench behind the targets where two turds were assigned to each target. Buffalo Butt and I were assigned to Target No. 35.

"One of you will pull the target down when you see a hole in the target. The other will take this," the coach held up a black cardboard disc with a dowel pin in the middle, "and insert it in the hole when the shooter hits in the white. You take a white one if he hits in the black. Raise the target. You will then take the disc," he pointed to a pole with a white metal circle on it, "and show the location of the hole."

The target was in a wooden frame about eight feet square that ran up and down rails on chains.

We heard the range officer on the PA system on the firing line advising the shooters to commence firing. We heard a sporadic sound like popping popcorn. We scanned our target. Did our turd fire yet? Did he miss the whole target?

Crack!

"*Jesus*," yelped Buffalo Butt, crouching. "Was that ours?"

Pulling the butts.
Photo courtesy of United States Marine Corps.

"I sure as hell hope so," I agreed, "cause if they get any closer, I'm on the deck!"

"Where's the hole, where's the goddamm hole," the Butt panicked, "I don't see no goddamm hole! Should I pull the dammed thing down?"

"Yeah, let's pull it down and see if we can see something. Maybe it's a pretty small hole."

Buffalo Butt yanked the target down and we scoured the surface, looking for the hit.

The field phone at our side rang. Brrrrrr! Brrrrr!

"You get it," Buffalo Butt gestured.

"Why should I get it? It's probably not even for us." I countered. "It's probably a wrong number."

"It might be Snake," the Butt suggested.

I grabbed the phone and held it to my ear.

"Target 35, Private Joyce speaking, sir!"

"Well, Private Joyce, are you going to give Shooter Number 35 a chance to take a shot, or are you on strike back there," a laconic voice asked.

"Yes, sir! I mean, no, sir! We thought he already shot, sir, and we were looking for the hole!"

"Just get the goddammed target back into the air! You'll know when a shot hits the target!" Click.

"Aye, aye, sir! Goodbye, sir!"

"He didn't even shoot yet," I screamed at the Butt. "Get the goddammed thing back in the air!"

Buffalo Butt gave a mighty shove and the target bounced off the retaining stops at the top, the entire frame quivering.

"Holy shit," the Butt marveled, "that damn thing moves up easily!"

The target finally quit shaking and we imagined our shooter taking deadly aim. We crouched in the bottom of the trench, awaiting the shot.

Kkkerrrackk!

"Jesus," Buffalo Butt moaned, "these sonfabitches are bad!"

"Never mind that," I yelled, "just get the dammed thing down here and let's find the hole!"

We frantically searched the target and found the hole in the 3-ring.

"A black spotter," I yelled to the Butt, "we need a black spotter! Quick!"

I jammed the black spotter in the hole and the Butt ran the target back up into the air. I grabbed the location disc and held it over the black spotter on the target. Just to make sure they saw it, I pumped the disc up and down a couple of times in front of the spotter.

Brrrrrrr!! Brrrrrrrr!

"The damn phone again. We must have a party line. Your turn," I handed the phone to the Butt.

"No, you take it," he whispered, "you're good at that shit."

"Target Number 35, Private Joyce..."

"Yeah, yeah," Mr. Laconic drawled, "I *knew* it had to be fucking Joyce! I know you two clowns are excited back there, but hold the dammed disc in *one* place and that's *over* the spotter! You're not a cheerleader at a pep rally!" Click.

"Yes, sir. You bet your ass, sir. Goodbye, sir." I advised the silent phone and hung up.

"Jesus, Joyce," Buffalo Butt cringed, "you didn't say that shit! We're gonna get into trouble."

"Hey," I calmed him, "it's all right. We talk all the time."

Buffalo Butt and I soon got the hang of it, finding the new hole, licking and pasting a sticker on the old hole, plugging the spotter in the new hole, running up the target and disking the spotter. We got short breaks when we and the shooters moved back to the 300-yard line, then finally to 500 yards.

While we were diligently searching our target for new holes from the 500-yard line, when the wooden frame on the right side of the target screamed and threw off a few splinters.

Buffalo Butt ripped the target frame down and I pounded a black spotter in the new hole in the wooden frame.

Brrrrrr! Brrrrrrr! The phone rang as we hoisted our wounded charge back into the air.

"Target Number 35, Private Joyce speaking," I drawled in my best laconic tone.

"Are you people all right back there," Mr. Laconic inquired nervously, "that last round hit the frame!"

"Yes, sir, the round impacted just outside the 2-ring. I'm disking it now."

I held the disc steadily in the air to the right of the target frame, although I was tempted to give the disc a few pumps to tell the shooter to get his shit together.

After pulling butts, we fired two other weapons for familiarization: the .45 Caliber pistol and the Browning Automatic Rifle, or "BAR."

The awesome BAR had two settings: "F" for "Fast" and "A" for "Awful Fast." I watched this automatic weapon closely as it might have a mind of its own and start spraying the area. They were carefully locked up at night, possibly to prevent the thing from waking up and running amok while you slept.

Hi Honey, Here I am!

After each day's firing, we were herded to the cleaning racks, lines of wooden tables where we ran bore cleaner though the barrel, disassembled, and brushed our brothers, U.S. Rifles, Caliber 30, M1.

Buffalo Butt and I finished sprucing up our brothers and waited by the road for the rest of the platoon. Two smiling girls driving by in a red Chevy convertible immediately captured our attention. Girls were a rare commodity.

"Hi Honey," Buffalo Butt yelled, "here I am!"

The smiling girls waved but kept going.

"And 'hi Honey, here *I* am,'" Snake's voice boomed from behind us. Sonofabitch! Last time we saw him was on the other side of the cleaning racks. How had he gotten all the way across the field without us seeing him? If Snake was indeed a reptile he had to be a Sidewinder.

"That was the most *romantic* thing I've ever heard. Is that the way you pick up girls?" Snake fluttered his eyelids, then pushed his chin in the Butt's face. "You do *not* address the civilians! You do not say shit to anyone! Go lock up your weapon and bring back the G.I. can. Go!"

Buffalo Butt double-timed back to the Quonset hut and returned with the can.

"On your head."

Buffalo put the king-sized bucket over his head. The can came down over his hips and rotated until the Butt put his hands up to support the can on his head.

"What did you say to those civilians? Let's hear it."

"Sir, Hi Honey, here I am," came a muffled voice.

"Can't hear you, Casanova."

"Sir, Hi Honey, here I am", a metallic voice echoed.

"You will patrol the length of the log fence and back. Stay inside the fence. We wouldn't want some civilian to run over our walking tin can, would we? You will wave at any vehicle that honks its horn. Forward, Harch!"

Buffalo carefully picked his way up to the fence.

"Garbage Can, Halt! Right, face! When you come to the end of the fence you will halt, about face, and march to the other end. There you will halt, about face, and keep going until I tell you otherwise. Forward, Harch!"

The garbage can detail marched off, a muffled hollow sound giving a continuous update of its current location. A car tooted his horn as it sped by and a hand slipped out from the bottom of the can and waved back and forth.

The Butt continued trolling for babes until chow, then resumed his vigil until dusk. Despite his efforts, no girls stopped to abduct him or give out their phone numbers. He lamented that the weight of the can probably made him an inch shorter.

Silk Skivvies

For three of the four days we had been firing in the final week at the range, I had scored 220 or more out of the possible 250 points. A score of 220 or more qualified a shooter as a "rifle expert." I dearly wanted that title and the silver badge with wreath and crossed rifles that went with it.

To heighten the pressure, Sgt. Snake told us he had bet Sgt. Frog of our sister platoon a case of beer that our platoon would have more "experts," more sharpshooters and more qualifiers than Frog's herd of turds. And that we had better not let him down.

As we marched to the range, I looked nervously at the sky, which promised rain. The wind seemed to gust. I worried that my carefully recorded rifle sight "dope" would be wrong. There were no practice shots. Every shot counted.

After firing from the offhand position, my score was a marginal forty-three. I needed an average of forty-four points from each of the five firing assignments to earn the Expert Badge.

Leaving the 200-yard line, I had amassed only eighty-seven points, still a point behind. Buffalo Butt, who had yet to qualify with 190 points all week, fired a seventy-five, also a point behind the required seventy-six to be on schedule for the Marksman Badge.

The 300-yard line was a little trickier as the wind got into it, gusting when the range officer gave permission to fire. We could see the little range flags on the target line whipping to the left, then falling limp. On "record day" we weren't allowed to ask the range coaches for estimated windage adjustments and were on our own.

I decided to wait until the wind died before squeezing off the ten slow fire shots and placed them carefully. I was one of the last two completing slow fire but got a forty-six, giving me a total of 133. Now I was one point ahead of the game.

Next, the ten rounds on rapid fire, in which we had to fire all ten rounds in less than a minute. I decided to add a click of windage since the gusts were picking up.

As the order came to "with a clip and two rounds, lock and load," my heart was pounding in my chest. I could feel drops of sweat coursing down my underarms. What if the windage was too much? Would I stitch the right side of the target, all in the 3-ring?

"Commence firing," the range officer shouted, and fifty U. S. Rifles, Caliber .30, M1 blasted away. There was no time to change windage or to wait until the gusts died. I just lined up the target, squeezed off the rounds and prayed.

The target came up slowly, telling the sad results in advance. A forty! I had really blown it! All the shots were on the right side of the target. I didn't *need* any windage correction. Now I was *three* points behind! I had to get a forty-seven to make "expert!"

"You *are* going to fire "expert," aren't you, Joyce," Snake threatened.

"Yes, sir," I confirmed.

"You had *better!*"

We trudged to the 500-yard line, many turds worried about their scores. This was the only time for the next year that we would have a chance to fire and would have to live with our scores for that time. This was the score that would go into our records. This score would determine the badge we would wear on our uniform for an entire year.

I had fired in the high forties from the 500-yard line all week long, as it was my best position. I took pride that I could hit a little black circle the size of a dinner plate seven or eight times out of ten at a quarter of a mile. But *not* with wind gusts.

As I lay with the rifle pointed at the pinhead targets, Sgt. Snake patrolled the firing line, shouting what he thought were words of encouragement.

"You better hit that goddammed target, Numb One! You better fucking *qualify*, Buffalo Butt! You people better goddammed *not embarrass* me!"

I never saw anyone so scared he'd lose a case of beer. Or that a rival platoon would shame him and his turds. Unless that scared turd was me. My stomach was doing flip-flops and my armpits were now dripping, even if it was mid December.

My first shot was a "four." Not too bad except now I had to hit the bulls eye seven times out of the next nine shots.

The second and third shots were both good hits in the "dinner plate." The fourth was another "four." I could have only one more "four." Then, three more bulls eyes.

The eight shot was disked as a "four." My stomach wrenched and my armpits now soaked my utility shirt. I now needed *two* bulls eyes. I could see Snake scoping out my hits with binoculars, but otherwise saying nothing.

Shooting from a quarter of a mile.
Photo courtesy of United States Marine Corps.

I fired the ninth shot. A bull! Well, here it is: my career as a shooter on the last shot. I lined up the sights. A sand flea decided that that was the time to add a little suspense, by buzzing in my ear. He lit, and started gnawing on my inner ear. I felt the pinch of his bite as I tried to concentrate on the shot. Hurry up and take your bite!

Out of the corner of my eye, I could see Snake fold his arms and pace between the two neighboring firing positions. If he yells at me to hurry up, honest to God, I'll give him a chance to do a little soft shoe. Tap dance him all the way to the end of the firing line.

Breathe, aim, hold, squeeze, I commanded myself. When this shot is fired, I'm going to reach up and murder the little winged jackhammer in my ear, regardless of what Snake does. Okay, here goes.

I carefully lined up the sights again, held my breath until the wind gust died and squeezed off the shot. I immediately stuck my trigger finger in my ear and took great satisfaction in smearing the little bastard all over my inner ear.

Snake probably saw me but was trained on my target with his binoculars. The target stayed down. And stayed down. Ohhmigod! It couldn't be a "Maggie's' Drawers," in which a red flag was slowly waved to show that the shooter had missed the *entire target!*

Slowly the target rose into the air. A tiny white spotter showed at the nine 'o clock position of the bulls eye! I had scored 220! A goddammed *expert!* I turned my head to see Snake's reaction.

He slowly lowered his binoculars and pointed at me.

"You lucked out this time, Joyce," he growled, and went to harass some other poor turd. Not much pomp and ceremony for my first Attaboy.

When the shooting was over, Snake and the other DI compared scores and it was determined that Snake owed the Frog a case of beer. Snake stalked over to our herd, red-faced.

"This is the worst bunch of shooters I've ever had as a drill instructor! Only four Experts, eleven Sharpshooters, fifty-three Marksmen, and *seven* of you pussies couldn't even *qualify* for Chrissakes! Ten-hut! Right, face! Awwworrdd, harch!"

We were marched to the PX, where only the

Unmagnificent Seven went into the building with Snake. Each came out with a small bag.

"You pussies that didn't qualify reach into your bag and take out your *badges*! If you're going to *be a pussy*, you're going to *look like a pussy*! Put them on!"

The miserable turds reached into their bags and each pulled out a pair of pink ladies silk panties.

"*On top* of your utilities, you dumb shit," Snake screamed at a turd that was unbuckling his utility trousers.

After our pussies were clad in their new underwear, Snake paraded the platoon up and down the nearby streets to model their new finery. Buffalo Butt, I'm pleased to report, was not among them, having fired a 192, two points over the minimum. I don't think ladies panties come in size 42, anyway.

Later that evening, SSgt. Sword called me and the other three highest shooters to his Quonset hut to offer us positions as rifle coaches on the range. We could stay on Parris Island and finish our enlistments there. All declined.

The pink skivvies market, as applied to non-qualifying turds, has apparently fallen off drastically since I was a marksmanship student. In 2003, 99.82% of the male recruits and 97.19% of the females qualified at the rifle range. Recruits are now given more than one chance, however, to qualify.

CHAPTER 16 – FINAL PHASE

A Night at the Beach

Shortly after we returned from the rifle range, we were again run out of Dodge for an excursion to Elliott's Beach. An overnight bivouac sounded pretty good to me. How bad could it be; being halfway between Myrtle Beach and Daytona? Maybe we could pick up some shells.

First, we had an equipment inspection, in which we laid out everything we were taking on a blanket on the parade ground. Helmet, canteen, rifle, poncho, tent pegs, shelter half, etc.

The shelter half was half a tent. If you showed up without yours or your buddy showed up without his, how could you sleep in half a tent? What if your buddy didn't show up? What if you had two right-sided halves or two left sided halves? It would be like playing Beach Blanket Bingo without Annette. I lost a lot of time worrying about things like this.

But I didn't see any half commodes or half chamber pots. Did they really mean what they said about being half-assed Marines?

Anyway, we re-packed all of our 782-gear in our backpacks, rolled up our shelter halves and blankets and stood ready to road test the platoon.

SSgt. Sword always gave us a "right, face" with the Big End facing front and leading the platoon. This time, however, he gave us a "left, face" and we on the Little End faced forward.

"Guidon to the front!" Our flag bearer raced around the platoon and took his position to the right front of the leading rank.

"The Little End has eaten dust so far, but today they're going to lead the platoon to Elliot's Beach. You people will take a full 30-inch step or get run over by the Big End. All right. Listen up. Forward Harch!"

We on the Little End, not used to such responsibility, surged on. With a cloud of dust and a mighty mental cry of "Hi, Ho, Shitbirds," we took off at a gallop, taking giant steps so that the thundering herd did not run us down.

"I told you people on the Little End to take 30-inch steps; you're not pulling the fucking Budweiser beer wagon!"

"What the hell are you carrying, Novak, a cow bell? What's rattling in your gear?"

After a mile or so, Sword decided that we dwarfs in the Little End weren't leaders after all, and switched back to the Big End leading.

The road was no more than two ruts in a 6-mile field of sand, complete with puddles and scattered debris. This was definitely the road less traveled.

Cpl. Winston, eager to fertilize new fields, accompanied us on the four-mile march. He trotted alongside, in front of, and between ranks of the platoon. Because of his height, I thought he should march with the Little End, but I guess rank had its privileges. He was also not taking a 30-inch step.

Once, Winston got entangled between the legs of a couple of heavily burdened recruits and growled and snapped just like the drill instructors. I saw one foolish recruit fake a kick at his bony ass, but Winston eluded the kick and trotted away, growling.

Hoot occasionally called out marching cadence to help pass the time. "Double time, harch! - I don't know but I've been told, Eskimo pussy is mighty cold!" Winston joined in, howling his accompaniment.

Out for a stroll to the beach.
Photo courtesy of United States Marine Corps.

"That was wonderful, girls. That sounded like Moonlight on the fuckin' Ganges!"

Gooney Bird managed to trip over his rifle, jamming the butt into his wedding tackle. He scrambled to his feet and limped along, but none the worse for wear. We needed a tenor anyway.

I found out later why we didn't pack half-commodes. To keep Marines from becoming as expensive as Wing Wipers in the Air Force, we lived off the land. A simple, yet ingenious, facility known as a "slit," or "straddle," trench was dug for every ten men.

The idea was to squat and relieve yourself over a ditch in the wilderness. In late December, you could get frostbite of the butt. There weren't many takers.

Once the exercise was over, we filled in the trench, noticing the vegetation grew like mad in adjoining little strips. We also observed that Cpl. Winston didn't use the slit trench as required.

We learned other fine points of field sanitation, using the slit trench and "catholes." A "cathole" turned out to be sort of a circular slit trench intended for one man. Maybe these were the "Officers' heads." We also learned to select the campsite with the prevailing wind blowing away from the tents and towards the slit trenches and catholes.

Elliott's Beach was a disappointment. It was simply a place where the water came up to an area of sand, pine trees, and sand fleas. A few primitive facilities such as a "water buffalo" for drinking water and bleachers where we had classes, showed that people had been there before, but probably suffered the same fate as early Colonial settlements.

Sword marched us to a long series of plywood racks, gave us a "right face" and ordered us to lay the rifles on the racks. We then blindfolded each other and stood at attention, half expecting to be shot. I sadly remembered my last meal had been horse cock, but no cigar. But Sword ordered us to disassemble our rifles and our hands flew gratefully to the task. We then reassembled the rifles and were granted a reprieve. I had come a long way from always having pieces left over when I reassembled anything, including a 4-legged table, in civilian life.

We learned to carry fingernail polish to suffocate ticks that we might pick up in the boondocks. After painting the varmint, we then were to take a bath in Tide. I vaguely remembered taking baths in civilian life, but the Corps didn't seem to own any bathtubs.

My worries about half of a tent were needless, as I was paired with another turd that was similarly worried. We hooked our two halves together, stepped the poles and had a little home away from home in short order. We dug a little ditch around the tent in case it rained, and lay on ponchos to keep the dampness from coming up from the ground. I also learned not to touch the roof of a wet tent when it was raining because that turned a drip into a dribble into the tent all night long.

It was a chilly night and one blanket didn't make the grade. Two sets of skivvies didn't seem like much of a help, so I slept in my field jacket. In the Marine Corps' ever-constant effort to save the taxpayers money, the Corps had a unique scarf called a towel. An ordinary bath towel was rolled, slipped around the neck, and tucked into your shirt or field jacket. I used that, too.

Shaving outside with cold water on a late December morning was invigorating. Since I was eighteen and could still get away with not shaving every day, I didn't bother to put a blade in the razor and was quickly finished.

I was a happy camper when the expedition was over and we were on the way back to Dodge City and warm barracks.

A Pillaging We Will Go

Now that we had fired our weapons for record and were in no danger of losing our precious sighting "dope," we fitted them with bayonets and stabbed straw and rag filled dummies. We ran howling across fields to attack immobile enemies, thrusting, slashing, and stabbing using vertical and horizontal butt strokes, the slash, and the thrust, while protecting ourselves with the guard, high port and parry positions.

Dumbo screamed and ran full tilt toward an unsuspecting and comatose rag "enemy." His bayonet clanged off the wooden supporting structure and Dumbo's momentum carried him through the structure, flattening both the rag dummy and the support pole.

"Try not to hold anything back, Dumbo," Snake encouraged, "the only problem is we're not going to play football with the enemy! You don't *tackle* him; you stick him with your bayonet!"

Dumbo was already on his feet, lining up his next wide receiver.

In the battle with the rigid piñatas, Dumbo was our only casualty. After we raced around the field a couple of times, raping and pillaging the dummies, the bayonet instructor called us over to review the fine points of hand to hand fighting.

"Success with the bayonet is ninety percent aggressiveness," he advised. "An onrushing, screaming Marine with cold steel on the end of his rifle has caused many an enemy to turn tail and run!"

It was the other ten percent I wondered about.

"Are there any questions so far," he asked.

"Sir, what is the other ten percent?"

"The other ten percent *what*," he frowned. Apparently, no one ever asked him questions.

"Sir, success with the bayonet is ninety percent aggressiveness. How can the private learn the other ten percent?"

"Good *training*, turd! Training is the other ten percent! That's what you're getting right now!"

"Okay," he looked around, "I need a volunteer to review the basic movements!" He pointed at me. "That's *you*, Ten Percent! Get a pugil stick, get suited up, and get out here!"

Damn, damn, and goddamm! Me and my big mouth! I ran to grab a pugil stick, a broom handle with large heavy pads on both ends. I struggled into the "armored bikini," a sort of padded chastity belt, a helmet, and boxing gloves. The instructor grabbed a pugil stick, but did not suit up.

"The first movement, you recall, is the *Jab*," he announced, as he speared me in the chest with such force that I flew backwards onto my butt.

"On your feet, Sweetcheeks," he instructed.

As I climbed back to my feet, I wondered where the protection was for the chest. Or for the stomach, or the shoulders, or the arms or the legs.

"The next movement is the *Slash*," he continued, as the end of his pugil stick blurred and found a home on the side of my helmet. Ask a question. Ask a question. No wonder he didn't get any questions.

"When your opponent is close enough that you can see his eyes, move quickly toward him, bare your teeth like a German Shepherd, and scream as loud as you can! Screaming is a great psychological advantage! Always scream when you attack!"

Upon which he screamed like a banshee, stepped forward and beat the shit out of me with the stick. He drew back, holding his stick at the "guard," or defensive position.

"Well, then," he inquired, "does that answer your question about the ten percent?"

I yessired to show I was a good sport. I understood that hitting your opponent when he wasn't ready was at least nine out of the ten percent.

"Okay, Ten Percent," he motioned to the instructor training our rival platoon, "let's see if you learned anything!"

A snarling hulk of a turd lumbered over, twitching and jerking like he was having spasms. He was so psyched up he probably would have taken on the instructor. He was "small," though, only about six foot two and easily 200 pounds. He could have been six foot six and 250 pounds. At five foot eight and 150 pounds I wasn't in the middleweight or even the light weight class. I was in the "one-size-fits-all" class.

"Get up there," the instructor shoved us both onto an elevated square of dirt. No ropes, no mat, no referee. No hope. Joyce, Joyce, he's our man, if he can do it – *anybody* can.

"Over there," he pointed at four large eager looking turds with pugil sticks waiting in a gully, "is the Goon Squad. If I think you guys aren't trying, I will blow my whistle twice and they will rush over here and beat the shit out of *both* of you!"

We stepped up onto the mound and the instructor, impatient shit that he was, immediately blew the whistle.

I started forward, bared my teeth like Cpl. Winston, and screamed. Before I could move, the Sasquatch clubbed me alongside my helmet with his stick, rattling my brains. Sonofabitch!

Stepping back, I bared my teeth again and got ready to scream, but Bigfoot came on fast, swinging his stick like a baseball bat. It was a slash, horizontal butt stroke and smash, all in one movement.

I pushed my stick up to high port to block any part of any stroke that I could, and his stick clanged against mine. I gave him three or four quick vertical butt strokes to his stomach, and he bent over. I remembered to scream and let him have as many horizontal butt strokes to the head as I could before he woke up and killed me. Instead, he dropped his stick and went to his knees. I was on him in a flash, giving him the "jab," baring my teeth and howling like a wolf.

"Okay, Okay! He's down, for Chrissakes," the instructor yelled, "get offa him!"

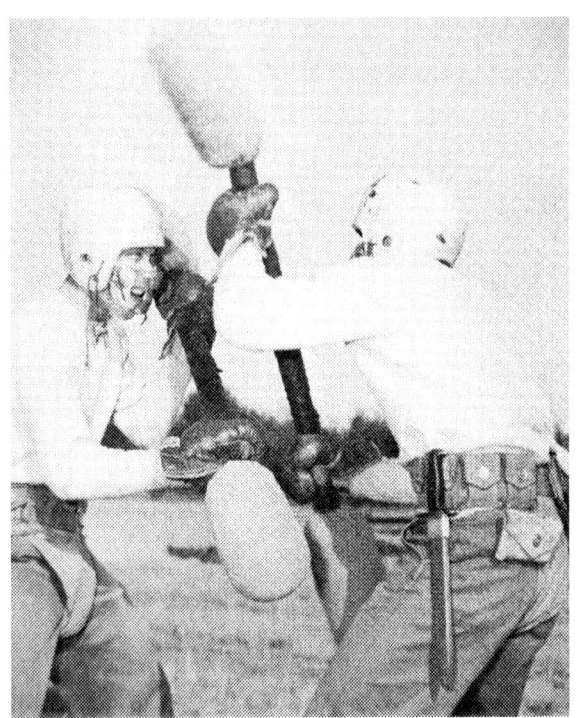

They say screaming helps.
Photo courtesy of United States Marine Corps.

In school, I had always been on the losing end of fist fights. My record was probably zero for seven. If I could get some rematches, I could now probably bat .500 or more with my trusty pugil stick.

"Next man, get suited up and get over here," the instructor waved. He didn't look my way.

I glimpsed Sgt. Snake eyeballing the Fallen Sasquatch, before he turned away, hiding a smile. I felt like I made Expert Rifleman all over again. So this is what a *real* Attaboy feels like!

McMAP. No, the recruits don't get "Happy Meals." The Corps has steadily refined its martial arts program to where both women and men receive training leading to a tan belt before they graduate basic. Throughout their Marine career they are afforded the opportunity and are encouraged to progress through black belt.

The Midnight Gardener

Once again, I was caught for smiling and I wondered if I really did have shit for brains. But this time there was something to smile about. We had been taken by bus to a hall where they told us if, on our upcoming 2-weeks leave we could talk a civilian buddy into joining the Corps, we could get another 2-week leave.

The catch was that we got a total of four weeks leave a year. This meant you got all of your leave at one time, instead of two weeks after boot camp, and the rest whenever you chose. Big deal. Big incentive. Hence, a knowing smile.

I had just returned to my seat on the bus to return to the barracks and remarked to my fellow turds what a little deal this was when, *Shazam!*, there was Sgt. Snake's leering face in front of my eyebrows.

"See me when we get back to the barracks!"

Not tonight, Snake, I mused to myself, I have a headache.

We didn't get back until taps but that didn't discourage the Snake.

"Joyce, you're fuckin' *incorrigible*," he began, "you can't learn, can you? You got *shit* for brains!"

Well, at least we agreed on my self-assessment. I stood there, awaiting his new cranial laxative to rid me of my affliction.

"Get your flashlight and come with me!"

I followed Snake out of the barracks and around back

to the swab racks, where an assortment of street brooms, mops, rakes and cleaning gear were stored. He grabbed a rake and thrust it into my hands.

"Get under there," he pointed to the 3-foot crawl space under our wooden barracks, "and rake every goddammed inch level!"

I ducked under the barracks and hunchbacked, started raking the dirt and sand.

"You will rake until you are finished. When you are done you will return the rake to the mop rack and hit the sack if you finish before reveille. You will *smile* the entire fucking time! I will inspect in the morning."

And he was gone.

The barracks was in the shape of a large "H" with the platoon squad bays on the long ends and the passageways with the drill instructors' hut in the connecting end.

I worked my way under the first squadbay, tidying up the dirt and sand, smiling all the way. Occasionally I inadvertently bumped the end of the rake on the surface above me, resulting in a sharp cracking sound.

After an hour or so, I worked my way down the short connecting leg under what I figured to be Snake's sleeping quarters. I *smiled* as I "inadvertently" pounded the hell out of his floor.

If I couldn't sleep with my strenuous schedule, then neither should he. Strutting around sticking his face into other people's faces couldn't take that much energy. After a half dozen accidental cracks, I moved on before I was tempted to give him a Gene Krupa drum solo.

Continuing on under my platoon's squadbay, I almost jumped out of my skivvies when I heard a growl only inches away. Maybe one of the gators or a dead recruit turned vampire was lurking in the shadows. My light shook as I turned it in the direction of the noise.

Lying on his side, lifting his head to watch me warily, was Corporal Winston.

"Good evening, Sir," I greeted him, smiling.

"Aaaarrrrvvvlll," he grumped and laid his head back on the sand.

As I approached, I could swear I could smell beer on his breath. A hard night out on the town drinking and skirt chasing, no doubt.

"Are you all right, sir," I asked, feeling foolish.

"Awwwrrrlll." I took that to mean not great.

I cautiously reached over and patted him gently on his big head.

He continued to growl softly but made no move to bite me in the ass or elsewhere. The poor guy was really hung over. I really liked dogs but this one was a non commissioned officer in the Marine Corps. I wasn't allowed to touch him. Time to move on.

"Cpl. Winston" lounging in his quarters.
Photo courtesy of United States Marine Corps.

"Well, sir," I advised, "the private needs the corporal to move so I can rake under you. The private needs to rake every inch under the barracks."

Winston made no move.

"Sir...." I began and stopped, because Winston started to snore, accompanied with snorts and vibrating jowls. His back legs started quivering and I knew he was off and running to an appointment with a nocturnal love.

I carefully raked around the little boozer and moved on to finish up the rest of the barracks. I hoped Winston wouldn't disturb too much of my manicuring effort with a spirited amorous dream or by answering the Call of Nature.

Cpl. Winston's Deposit

"Jesus Christ! Sonofabitch," Snake screamed from the hall in front on the DI hut. "Goddammit," he continued, "House Mouse! Get your furry ass in here! *Now!*"

Private Sterling, the House Mouse, sped to the scene amidst our chorus of "Private Sterling, report to the drill instructor!"

"Fire Watch! Get in here! All fire watches for last night, get in here! *On the double!*"

Who's next, I thought, all the King's men?

"What the hell is this," Snake demanded of the House Mouse.

Sterling looked down at the polished wooden deck.

"Sir, it looks like dog shit," Sterling ventured.

"Firewatch, how did this get here?"

"Sir, the firewatch doesn't know," the four firewatches chorused.

Its okay, Sarge, I thought. It's not a *grenade*. It

won't *explode*. There's no hurry. There are truly enough turds for us all. You, Snake, go get your bucket.

I didn't know why Snake didn't check up on Cpl. Winston's whereabouts and whether the good corporal had an alibi, but that was too logical. Maybe he could fingerprint the turd and match it to one of us turds. Sort of a chip off the ole block, so to speak.

We turds suspected the culprit was Sgt. Frog. Frog's platoon had lost the latest competition between the platoons and he was a sore loser. It would have been easy to smuggle in the turd while the fire watch was making his rounds in the rear of the squadbay. The firewatch probably would have been a willing co-conspirator anyway.

Or, since Winston probably had shit for brains, too, the good Corporal may have just dropped by to give a Snake a piece of his mind.

Snake stared up at the overhead, where Sgt. Frog's DI hut occupied the space directly above.

Since tidying up the DIs' hut was the House Mouse's duty, he was delegated to dispose of the turd in an appropriate manner. Whether this meant returning the turd to its probable owner, or placing it on the front seat of Sgt. Frog's Henry J, Snake didn't say.

How Ya Gonna Keep 'Em Down On the Farm?

With only two days to graduation, SSgt. Sword described the various duty assignments that we might expect after completing the four weeks in the Infantry Training Regiment at Camp Geiger, North Carolina.

"Some of you will be assigned to embassy duty or sea duty aboard ship. Embassy duty and sea duty are two of the best duty slots."

"For those of you going to Camp Lejeune, you'll

probably end up in the FMF, or Fleet Marine Force. They are also known as the 'Fighting Mother Fuckers.'"

"At last," Private Washington, a black recruit from Scranton whispered, "a place for me."

"There is also Recon," SSgt. Sword continued, "but that is for Marines with a little time in the Corps. It is one of our best outfits. A bunch of *bad* motherfuckers."

Yea, though I walk through the valley of the shadow of death, I will fear no evil, for I am the baddest motherfucker in the valley.

"Those of you who have not been specifically assigned to a school such as aviation or electronics will be assigned based on the recommendations of your drill instructors. Those of you that have worked the hardest, are the most squared away, and have the most potential to succeed will be awarded the best assignments."

He stored his clipboard under his arm and stood up.

"Following this meeting, those recruits who think they deserve to be considered for any of these, or any other assignments, will present themselves, one at a time, at my hatch."

Thereafter followed a short line of recruits, desiring to make know their preferences. I didn't go, figuring that I would be posted to El Bongo Island or some other similar wretched paradise anyway.

Private Kechler, a tall, squared away recruit knocked on the pine.

"Sir, Private Kechler requests permission to speak to the drill instructor!"

"Speak," said Sword.

"Sir, Private Kechler requests consideration for assignment to Sea School!"

"Your request is noted. Dismissed!"

Kechler would probably get it too, because he was a hard worker, the third squad leader, and helped keep other recruits out of trouble.

The next applicant, one Abraham Goldenstein, a.k.a. Moses, knocked forcibly on the hatch frame. Private Goldenstein was a red-faced, bug-eyed recruit that always seemed out of breath as though he had just completed a 5-mile run. Although he was reasonably fit, he still had a small potbelly and a double chin that became taut only when he lifted his chin. He lifted his chin most of the time.

"Speak," growled Sword.

"Sir, Private Goldenstein requests assignment to Recon!"

"What," said the astonished Sword, coming out into the passageway. "What makes you think you can cut the course at Recon?"

"Sir," Goldenstein screamed, "I'm a bad *motherfucker!*"

"No, not yet, you're not," Sword said, not unkindly. "Get the fuck outa here."

"Aye, Aye, sir," Abie shrieked, did an about face and marched back to the squadbay, his double chin clearly visible.

Gooney Bird and his cohort then requested posting as brig guards, as they thought they would be more comfortable in familiar surroundings. Requests denied, with advice they stay as far away as possible from the penal system.

Dumbo requested assignment to radio school where his oversize ears might be put to advantage listening to radio transmissions. Request denied, with advice that he use his ears to simply listen for orders, and to be grateful that he wasn't ordered to repeat recruit training.

Weezil had the effrontery to request posting to Officers Candidate School at Quantico. Sword advised that OCS was booked for the next four years and that they would have to get along without him somehow.

Cpl. Winston was apparently happy with his present assignment and didn't show.

For He's A Jolly Good Fellow

On Christmas Day, we were still boots. We knew twelve weeks were up the next day and thought maybe that the Marine Corps would graduate us a day early. But it seemed that the Corps needed seventy-four more armed killers to repel a possible invasion of Parris Island on Christmas Day.

It wasn't such a bad day, though. There were no turtle doves, partridges in pear trees, or French hens. Maybe one of the drill instructor's wives would drop off some cookies. We didn't hang stockings, exchange presents, or have a tree, but we did sing Christmas carols to the drill instructor. Sgt. Gibson had the duty.

One of his favorites were "For He's a Jolly Good Fellow" which we sang three or four times. We didn't know if the "jolly good fellow" was Jesus Christ, Saint Nick or, perhaps, good ole Sgt. Gibson. Most of us didn't know all the words but Hoot seemed satisfied.

We followed through with "All I want for Christmas is my two front balls" and, of course, all three verses of the Marines' Hymn.

We had a great meal at afternoon chow but the highlight of my Christmas was calling home. No one else did, as far as I know. A window of opportunity arose when Hoot retreated to his hut and let us have most of the afternoon to write letters, and to shine our shoes and brass.

I took off across the field to the Triangle PX, where they had an outside pay phone. I called my Mom and Dad and wished them a 3-minute Merry Christmas before I ran a scorching return to the barracks.

After evening chow, Hoot had us wish the civilized world a "Merry Christmas and to all, a good night." We then turned toward General Hauling's house and wished him Merry Christmas. My heart wasn't in it as he was still on my shit list for not coming to welcome us at the train station.

I'm Pretty Sure I'm Confident

The next morning we went to the Confidence Course, a series of obstacles that everybody was going to overcome and thereby get some confidence.

Climbing over walls and swinging on ropes over ditches was easy. So was running along suspended telephone poles. The first really bad one was kind of a giant baby crib suspended on poles, about 30 or 40 feet off the ground. A sign correctly proclaimed that it was "The Tough One."

You had to climb up ropes just to get on the monstrosity, then run along widely spaced poles to get to the other side. The poles were spaced far enough apart that you had to start running and keep running in order to reach the next pole.

I looked down to the two or three feet of sawdust piled under the structure and hoped I wouldn't be visiting it soon. I committed to the run and made it to the large A-frame ladder on the other side.

Horizontal logs were placed further apart until you got to the top where a rope was suspended to the ground. I climbed onto the first and barely reached the second. I hauled myself up on the second log but could not reach the third.

"Undo your rifle sling and loop it around the log! Pull yourself up," shouted Sgt. Gibson.

Sure, and rhinos can fly, I thought savagely. Why in the hell can't they make an obstacle for regular sized people?

On top of Ole Smokey.
Photo courtesy of United States Marine Corps.

Trying not to look down, I unfastened the sling and looped it over Mt. Everest. I gotta get up there somehow. I pulled on the rifle and sling and somehow got up there.

Standing on the top rung I hugged the top of the frame. I still couldn't reach the exit rope. I leaned my foot out as far as it would reach but I still couldn't touch it. My stomach was doing flip-flops as I twisted and kicked thin air.

"We don't have all day, John Wayne," Gibson shouted up. Behind me, people were stacking up.

Finally, I leaned out and snapped the rifle sling around the rope, and drew it to my hand. It started to swing back and I frantically grabbed it with one hand, leaving the safety of the A-frame. I shot down the rope one handed like a firemen on a fireman's pole, hanging for dear life onto my best friend, U.S. Rifle, Caliber.30, M1, with the other. My short life flashed before my eyes and I had a vision of my body crumpling like an accordion upon impact, my ears growing out of my ankles. After landing in the sawdust with my hand on fire, Sgt. Gibson stood over me.

"You're supposed to hang on with both hands, Tarzan. You probably want to go round and try it again? Or do you want to go on to 'The Slide for Life?'"

I figured the "Slide for Life" would finish me off anyway so what did I have to lose?

"Sir, the private thinks he's ready for The Slide for Life!"

Wrong answer. Marines were supposed to kick ass and take names, not overcome obstacles in a half assed manner.

Sgt. Gibson took a long look at me, clearly disappointed that he wouldn't get to see another five-point landing. He waved me on to the Slide and gestured to Sgt. Snake, who sat atop a pole about fifty feet high. It could have been sixty, or maybe seventy feet.

The poles had steps, at least, and had a cable strung from its top across a lake to a stubby ten-foot pole on the opposite side. The temperature was a bit nippy, causing steam to rise from the water. Inviting looking damn thing.

A recruit was moving hand over hand, his legs wrapped around the cable toward the lower far end.

"Well, get up here, Joyce," Snake bellowed down, "unless you intend to *walk* across!"

Smart ass. I climbed up the pole, my heart thudding in my chest. I never liked heights, let alone Sgt. Snake or the prospect of swimming in December. It seemed like the steps would never end but I finally reached the top. Snake yelled to get on to the cable and start down.

The steel cable was as cold as a well digger's ass but somewhat helped cool my still smarting hand. It was slow going as my body weight, as well as my rifle, canteen and helmet sagged on the cable. Looking down at the other pole, I saw that I had made about 40 or 50 feet of progress. Another hundred feet to go. I was about forty feet above the steaming morass.

"Hurry up," Snake growled, grabbing the cable and rotating his arms. I hugged the cable with a death grip with both hands as it whooshed in a ten-foot arc. The centrifugal force threatened to throw me off at any second.

I redoubled my efforts and pushed down the cable twenty or thirty more feet. I saw that I was very near the halfway point. I started again.

"I said hurry up, Joyce," Snake yelled and gave the cable a couple of vicious rotations. The cable and I made a couple of twenty-foot circles as I saw the water going by about thirty feet away, then the sky.

I knew I was a goner as the last ride had taken almost all of my remaining strength. It was all I could do to hold on, let alone go for another loop. On my next revolution, I threw my rifle as far as I could to the nearest bank. My helmet went on the next. At the top of my next circle I simply let go and hoped for a passing by Flying Wallenda. I floated on air for an instant; then plummeted like a lead turkey.

The frigid water punched my breath away as I drifted into the bottom. A sucking, oozing, bottom. I stood up, dragging one leg after another through the quagmire until I reached the bank. I retrieved my rifle and helmet and stood with about twenty other recruits who had also been slingshot off the cable. A mist rose from our huddling, yearning mass, our wet clothing steaming in the chill.

Recruit on his way down to the drink.
Photo courtesy of United States Marine Corps.

Splash. Photo courtesy of United States Marine Corps.

"You people will get your gear together and double time back to the barracks. Get your clothes off, take a hot shower and clean your rifles and gear. Git!"

The Confidence Course had done its job. I was confident I could get back to the barracks and take a hot shower.

For a long time I was embarrassed for having gone down the Slide for Life cable so slowly that I was shaken off. Over the years, however, almost every PI graduate I've spoken to admitted that he too, went into the water.

And although some parts of the Confidence Course are tough, its not in the same category as the grueling 54-hour "Crucible" exercise. Recruits march forty miles and must use teamwork to solve combat problems while getting only eight hours sleep and two and a half "meals-ready-to-eat."

My Report Card

Although I would not graduate valedictorian, I thought I had done well at Pushup University. I had joined an outfit that takes pride in setting records, like unloading a train or busload of civilians in the dark in thirty seconds, although that may not be the outfit's personal best time.

I had survived the Marine Corps' treatment of a new platoon of taking it by the scruff of the neck and molding it into a team of lethal "yessirmen." I had not only survived the twelve weeks of "shock and awe" but had also gained some wide and diversified experience in practical and career-enhancing skills such as:

1. **Learning how to be economical** – the fine points of mowing the lawn with a sharp knife and bucket. Extra credit for riding antique buffers to get that truly shiny floor. Give myself an "A."

2. **Developing close personal relationships** - adopting and bonding with my brother and best friend, US Rifle Caliber .30. M1. Another "A."

3. **Learning a foreign language** – marching to the famous "Darrell Dottle" DI Cadence for which there is no Dottle-to-English Dictionary. Have to give myself a "C." (I grade on the "curve.")

4. **Becoming a gourmet** – applying Duncan Hines criteria to exotic foods such as SOS, boiled rat, and lizard sandwich. I think an "A" there.

5. **Protecting myself in sexual encounters** – understanding explicit visual aids such as cucumbers and condoms, and references to wheelbarrows. At this stage, ahem, I think an "Incomplete."

6. **Conducting myself at recreational events** – participating in blanket parties, field days, and holidays on asphalt. I think an overall "B+."

7. **Gaining experience in public speaking** – addressing marching troops from a reviewing stand and giving the eulogy for a sand flea. Absolutely an "A."

8. **Entering public service** – being a waiter and serving food to high ranking, but salty, bulldogs. Another "A."

9. **How to pick up girls** – observing in church, the "garbage can on your head" maneuver, and through letter writing campaigns. Partial success here, probably a "B+."

10 **Developing your body** – learning challenging exercises like "up and on shoulder locker box" and combating centrifugal force while traversing the "Slide For Life." Another "B."

11. **How to Strategize** – how to do the minimum number of "up and on shoulder" or "huff 'n puffs" without getting caught by the drill instructor. I believe a shameless "A."

12. **How to develop a sense of humor.** – snickering at drill instructor expressions of frustration and crude insults to fellow turds, again without getting caught. Alas, an "F," my only failing grade.

All in all, though, not too bad. I was now as tall as Snake, had a little tuft of hair under my dog tags, but most of all, I had a *pair*.

CHAPTER 17 – VENI, VIDI, VICI

My Pride Runneth Over

After peeling the muck from our clothes and faces, we had an hour to get ready for Graduation. For the first time, we would be wearing the dress shoes we had been spit polishing for twelve weeks. We strutted around the squadbay, sporting our tailored dress greens with our shooting badges.

The Graduation was indoors in an auditorium. The drill instructors looked sharp in their dress greens, complete with campaign ribbons and shooting badges.

After almost three months, this was the day we had lived for. It all came to this. All the King's horses and all the King's men *had* put Humpty Dumpty together again.

Each recruit's name was called by my old friend, the sergeant major, three stripes up and four stripes down with a star in the middle. We walked across the stage like at high school graduation and the Colonel pinned our Eagle, Globe and Anchors on the lapels of our dress greens.

"Congratulations, Marine!" They were the sweetest words I ever heard. My green dress blouse tightened as my chest swelled with pride. I had made it! I was no longer a pimple on a Marine's ass. Some turd was now a pimple on *my* ass.

One Marine, as we were no longer turds, won the "Blues Award," a full set of dress blues and also a PFC stripe. Hawkins, a truly squared away, helpful, hardworking, deserving guy, won the award.

Buffalo Butt and Dumbo were talking to Sgt. Snake in a cluster of Marines after the ceremony. I joined them.

"You know, Buffalo Butt and Dumbo, I had to put

you two through a lot of bullshit to get you two squared away. There were times when I never thought either of you would make it. But I'll tell you this. If ever the screaming hordes comes running over a hill with guns blazing, I'd be proud to have either one of you in my fighting hole."

Tears welled up in my eyes and for the umpteenth time in twelve weeks, I was sure I was going to blubber like a baby.

"And you, Joyce," he continued, "if you hadn't been such a clown and kept your eyeballs from wandering, you might have gotten a PFC stripe. You didn't get away with *everything* you thought you did."

"Thank you, sir," I said sincerely. I wondered if it was the "up and on shoulders" or the PX squat thrusts, but I had finally learned not to ask certain types of questions. "I appreciate what you've done for me."

And I meant it.

Hoot made a brief appearance, but didn't have much to say. After shaking everyone's hand and wishing him luck, he excused himself with tears in his eyes.

I was going to Sea School, one of the prize assignments. Maybe a smile here and there didn't hurt me as much as I thought. I had grown 2 ¾ inches and had moved up slightly from the Little End. I might even have leadership potential.

From the auditorium we marched for the last time to the grinder. Thirteen platoons were graduating, including one platoon of Women Marines, or "WMs."

Families of recruits were in the grandstand. Even the General showed up. Even though he didn't get up to welcome us at one in the morning twelve weeks ago, he was kind enough to see us off.

The swords of the officers and drill instructors glinted in the sun, as they took their positions to start the parade.

A lone officer stood in front of the reviewing stand, facing the thirteen platoons and their drill instructors.

"Pass in review," he shouted.

"Regiment! Battalion! Company! Platoon!" The commands rippled down to each succeeding smaller unit. "Right, *Face!*" Then after a pause, "Forward, *March!*"

The band started playing "Semper Fi" as it and the thirteen platoons stepped off as one. We were the seventh platoon in line, a very lucky number, I thought as my chest led the way. We marched up to the end of the parade field, turned left, and then turned left again to come down in front of the review stand. The last half-mile on the "Grinder."

The legs of almost a thousand recruits stepping as one, flashed left, then right. It looked like a giant centipede, having been taught to coordinate its many legs in precision.

Corporal Winston trotted along with our platoon, although it was hard to tell if he was in step. Having two left and two right legs, there was a chance he was right at least half the time.

He was dressed to the nines in his immaculately starched khaki uniform.

Passing in front of the reviewing stand, Staff Sergeant Sword sharply raised his sword in front of his face, then crisply down to his side.

"Eyes, *Right*," he commanded and we jerked our heads to the right toward the reviewing officer and review stand. Even Corporal Winston managed to turn his head and I felt a kinship with him.

The reviewing officer and the General returned Sword's salute.

"Ready, *front*," Sword commanded, and we again turned our faces to the front.

"Cpl. Winston strutting his stuff.
Photo courtesy of United States Marine Corps.

At that moment drums thundered, and the band broke into the Marines' Hymn. Chills cascaded down my back and tears welled in my eyes. I felt such a tremendous surge of pride and emotion; I could hardly keep from bawling like a baby.

I was one of *them*! The band was playing for *me*, as well as all the other Marines present. It was absolutely the *proudest moment* of my life. I once was lost, but now I am found.

After we had re-formed in front of the review stand, our guidons flags were surrendered, signifying that our platoons had completed training and were now out of existence. Platoon 2037, my home and my family for twelve weeks, was no more.

Corporal Winston, his job done for the morning, trotted off in the direction of the Second Battalion mess hall.

The Last Half Mile. Photo courtesy of United States Marine Corps

Having met several former and present-day DIs, I have a new respect of the men and women we loved to hate. DIs have to go through a twelve-week school and put in an average of 100 hours a week while training recruits. Read the book *The Few and the Proud* by Larry Smith to get an appreciation for these intrepid young men and women.

Give Me Liberty

Immediately following Graduation, we were given four or five hours base liberty to visit the PX, soda shop, or any other place on the base. I half expected Snake to propose that we instead go marching. Rejecting marching on the drill field, snapping in on the range, or going to PT, I headed for the "Gung Ho Jewelry Shop," a place where you could buy Marine Corps rings, lockets, bracelets, paperweights, and all kinds of good stuff.

Fanelli seemed to be trying to corner the sterling silver locket market, purchasing *seven* silver U.S. Marine Corps lockets. His replacements must have come through.

I bought a sterling silver ring with gold EGAs on the sides, *four* sterling silver lockets, a pack of cigars, and headed for the soda shop. I had come through, too, although Henrietta the majorette, Pat the cheerleader and Sweet Antoinette Number Two didn't make the cut.

There I bought a chocolate soda, drank less than half of it and promptly threw up. My body was apparently pissed for not having sweets or sugar in twelve weeks.

That evening, Sgt. Gibson took us to see a movie at the outdoor theatre. It was like a little drive-in, except with park benches instead of cars. Bob Hope did not post. Trust the Corps not to overspend on entertainment. We wore our towel scarves to keep out the cold.

We were to be liberated the next day, December 27th.

The Beat Goes On

Later the next morning, we were to leave by bus for Camp Geiger, a suburb of Camp LeJeune, North Carolina, for Infantry Training. A solemn SSgt. Sword assembled us in the squadbay for his farewell.

"You are now Marines. That's Marine with a capital "M". I know that many of you thought this day would never come." He paused, and allowed himself one of his rare smiles. "I wondered if it ever would, too."

"I'm proud of you all. Some of you have had to work a lot harder than others. I'd be proud to share a fighting hole with any of you. In fact, I'd be *confident* to share that hole with you. I know that every one of you would stand and face the enemy and fire your weapon."

"You are in a brotherhood that doesn't leave anyone behind. Until the day you die, you will be a Marine. And when you are relieved of duty and get your Final Orders to report to Heaven's Gate, you will meet the others who went before you; men from Iwo Jima to Frozen Chosin to members of this platoon."

"Sergeants Snake and Gibson and I have done our best. It's up to you now. For the next two or three, or twenty years, stay squared away, and take care of each other."

"Don't embarrass us." He allowed himself another rare smile.

"With your seabags and rifles, and at your *leisure*, get outside," SSgt. Sword told us for the last time. We walked, not ran, outside to await the buses. We stood in groups, talking and smoking, and just generally having a big tea party. Even smiling.

"I wonder if they'd let me take my bucket," Gooney Bird wondered, looking at the manicured grass in front of the barracks.

"Wow," Dumbo observed, "did you guys know these trees have Spanish Moss on them?"

"Why don't you and Dumbo get some for your buckets," Weezil suggested. Smartass to the end.

"Or maybe you'll need *yours*, Weezil," the King of the Turds chimed in, "in case Aunt Sally sends you some more cherries."

After a few minutes we noticed a surging horde of newly clad turds struggling down the street toward us. The horde walked, then ran, then slowed down again. Two drill instructors ran among their midst, barking and nipping at their heels like sheep dogs.

The staccato yells of "Pick up that bag! Close it up! Move it! Get off your knees, turd! Keep it closed up! You need help carrying that?" got closer and closer.

The horde panted and moaned its way down the street, punctuating their song with the scraping of dragged seabags on the asphalt. As they approached, we could see the white tags of newly issued utilities.

New kids on the block. Photo courtesy of the Parris Island Museum and the United States Marine Corps.

I remembered the sheer pain of getting my shins kicked in, the shoving of the seabags against my shoulders, panting for breath and muscles on fire. The chalk white and flushed faces of the terrified and panic stricken recruits streamed by.

As they started to pass us, the DI on the periphery turned to look at us, nodded slightly, and *winked*.

"Put those goddammed bags on your shoulders! Who told you to slow down? You bunch of pussies! Close it up or my size 12 will bring up the rear!"

Yeah, yeah. Same old shit.

A small recruit, destined for the Little End, stole a glance at us, sitting on our seabags on the lawn. His ashen face told volumes in the three Fs: fear, frustration and fatigue.

Could I have looked like that, only twelve weeks ago? Of course I did.

Don't worry, turd, I silently advised him. In seven or eight weeks, if you're still here, you'll be able to endure the severest tongue lashing and still have a second or two to think about your Wild Thing. You'll help lift a telephone pole, let alone a seabag, and run a mile with it. Look inward, look to Chesty, and you will prevail.

So will the turds with you and the ones after you. And the ones after them.

Parris Island is *forever*.

I try to attend at least one Parris Island graduation each year. When I do, I am acutely aware that every new graduate who sees me wishes me a "Good Morning, Sir!" I wish him or her in return, "Congratulations, *Marine!*" To see the pride and goodwill on each of their young faces is more than worth the trip.

Semper Fi, Marines.

End

Epilogue

Okay, now you've been there, done that. You've graduated and are, at least, an "armchair Marine." That's Marine with a capital "M." You've given them twenty, marched a few hundred miles, and suffered under some coarse language. Is this shit really *necessary*? Does the training work? Do you feel lucky? Well, you should feel a little more confident, but since you sat on your ass the whole way through the book, I doubt if you're any tougher.

Parris Island has changed since we graduated. The recruits still train for twelve weeks and shoot at targets a quarter of a mile away. Fear, or at least a healthy respect, is probably still the biggest motivator. The weapons have changed from M1 Garands to M16s and the WWII wooden barracks have been replaced with brick ones.

PI has also changed from being more Spartan and harsh to a kinder, gentler place. That's probably open to discussion from the more recent grads.

The Corps now has to work with the Nintendo generation instead of the farm boys, grocery baggers, and service station attendants of my day. They've had to change the physical training to adjust. That means *different*, not less. For example, three of the biggest changes have been the introduction of General Krulak's 54-hour Crucible, the Core Values (Honor, Courage and Commitment), and martial arts training.

A popular recruiting slogan years ago warned: "We don't promise you a rose garden." I've visited PI several times over the past few years and I can tell you, I still don't see any evidence of a rose garden. But no longer can a drill instructor use profanity and some of the other methods I've described in this book.

Momma's boys and sensitive young persons will still have a tough time of it. The question is: "If you were in a fighting hole (foxhole) and the screaming hordes came charging over the hill, would you want Momma's boy or Mr. or Ms. Sensitive protecting your back if he or she hadn't been sufficiently mentally toughened to do so?"

There will always be young men and women who choose to possibly put themselves in harm's way, similar to police officers and firemen. Knowing that someday they may be in combat helps them accept the tough training which is designed to keep them and their comrades alive.

We are presently engaged in a war, and now many of our young brothers and sisters *are in* harm's way. They have not been sent unprepared.

Core Values, the Crucible, and twelve weeks of training at Parris Island or San Diego, plus weeks of additional training at Infantry Training Regiment, has prepared them mentally, physically and morally. The outstanding record of the Marine Corps in Iraq and Afghanistan shows the effectiveness of that training.

The tenacity I learned in Parris Island enabled me to earn three college degrees. I've had four careers in electrical engineering, accounting, corporate finance, and securities brokerage, the last of which I was willing to bet on myself when every month started at zero income as a commission-only stock broker.

In the community, my Parris Island training helped me assume positions of leadership in my church, cub scouts, condo association, and the Marine Corps League.

Parris Island is one of the most visited military installations in the United States. What's the attraction? The Island has no towering ships or giant airplanes or battle tanks. What they *do have* is men and women. The people who visit are mostly families of graduating recruits and many, many Parris Island graduates.

We former graduates vie for a chance to sleep a night in the recruit barracks, eat in the mess hall with the recruits, and to stand on the famous "yellow footprints" for a ration of verbal abuse from the receiving drill instructors. Why do we do this? Well, shucks, I don't know; I guess it sort of makes us feel like going home again.

Some people still think Parris Island is a Devil's Island in which our tender young sons and daughters are mistreated, brainwashed and humiliated. Almost like working in a corporate environment. No one pictures recruits laughing. Let me tell you, they do. Not openly, as you've seen. I've never laughed in the boss's face either (except one time in which I was fired). *If you can laugh, things aren't hopeless.* I admit that I laughed more after I graduated. This is how it was. I laughed then, but now that I've written the book, I'm entitled to, and do, laugh myself sidesaddle.

Especially since my drill instructor was tougher than yours.

Glossary

The language of boot camp is unique and ageless. Some of these terms are unique to particular drill instructors but most will be familiar to Parris Island boots over the past forty or fifty years.

782 gear	field equipment such as cartridge belt, canteen, and bayonet
Aye, aye	acknowledgement of order
BAM	broad-assed Marine, Women Marine
Blivik, blivet	ten pounds of shit in a five-pound bag
Blouse	uniform coat, jacket
Bloused trousers	tucking in bottoms of trousers with blousing garters
Boiled rat	pot roast
Boondockers	shoes which cover the ankles, clodhoppers
Bug juice	sweetened, colored water served in mess hall
Bulkhead	wall
Butts	trench behind rifle range targets
Cadence	DIs rhythm to keep marching platoon in step
Candy Ass	slacker
Cat hole	a shallow basin scraped in the ground where human waste is deposited
Chow	food

Clap	gonorrhea, a.k.a. the Galloping Crud
Cosmolene	protective grease on rifle
Cover	hat, cap
Crumb catcher	mouth
D.I.	Drill instructor
Deck	floor
Doggie dicks	small sausages
Dope	Rifle sight settings
Dynamited chicken	Chicken a la King
EGA	eagle, globe and anchor, USMC emblem
Field day	clean up the barracks
Fisheyes	tapioca
Four Eyes	a recruit with eyeglasses
FUBAB	fucked up beyond all belief
FUBAR	fucked up beyond all repair
Green weenie	what the Corps screws you with
Grinder	drill field
Grunt	infantryman
Guide	recruit that carries guidon
Guidon	platoon pennant with platoon number
Gung ho	enthused, ready to kick ass and take names
Hatch	door
Head	bathroom
Horsecock	baloney, sandwich meat
Irish pennant	errant thread on uniform or equipment

Junk on the bunk	equipment and clothing laid out on the rack for inspection
Left	an important direction or foot, your other right
Lubriplate	lubricant to help protect rifle part from wear
Maggie's drawers	red flag indicating complete miss of target at rifle range
Marine	that's Marine with a capital M
Me	no such recruit in boot camp, neither is 'I'
Mess hall	a place where mess, or rather food, is served
NCO	non-commissioned officer
Oh dark thirty	after midnight but before civilized working hours
Oh dark ugly	earlier than oh dark thirty
Overhead	ceiling
POU	Psychiatric Observation Unit, mental hospital
PT	physical training, Pushup University
PX	post exchange, kind of military general store
Piece	Rifle, weapon
Police	clean up
Pogey bait	candy, pastry, sweets
Rack	bunk, bed
Recycle	repeat part of training with a junior platoon

Right	another important direction, your other left
Rosie	Rosie (sometimes Suzie) Rottencrotch, the wench most likely to give you the clap
SOS	creamed chipped beef on toast, Shit On a Shingle
Secure	finish up, stop activity, lock up
Semper Fidelis	always faithful, motto of the Marines
Shit sandwich	screwed up event
Sick bay	little hospital, dispensary
Skivvies	underwear, shorts and shirts
Sir	any person other than the boot, the drill instructor mostly, but also officers, barbers, instructors and even some dogs
Skuzzy	Smelly, dirty, sweaty, filthy
Slider	hamburger
Smile	there is no such thing in boot camp
Snap in	pretending to fire rifle without bullets, dry fire
Snot locker	nose
Sound off	give answer loudly, shout, scream
Soup sandwich	not good, sharp, crisp, not military
Squadbay	Spartan room with 75 double-decker racks
Square away	make neat, shape up
Slit trench	a rectangular grave for several human's waste

Standby	a warning that something was about to happen, like a drill instructor entering the squadbay
Swagger stick	neat little stick with bullet on one end and shell casing on other
Tea party	platoon running amok
The Position	a horizontal position of the body, suspended by the palms of your hands and your toes, ready for pushups
Throne	commode
Throne room	an open area of thrones without partitions or doors
Tube steak	baloney, horsecock
WM	Woman Marine
Water buffalo	water tank on wheels
Wedding tackle	the family jewels

Parris Island Reading List

The Few and the Proud. Marine Corps Drill Instructors in Their own Words. 2006 by Larry Smith.

Parris Island. Images of America. 2002 by Eugene Alvarez, Phd.

Into The Crucible. Making Marines for the 21st Century. 2000 by James Woulfe and James B. Woulfe.

Making the Corps. The story of boot camp Platoon 3086. 1997 by Thomas E. Ricks.

Boot. The Inside Story of How a Few Good Men Become Today's Marines. 1987 by Daniel Da Cruz.

Send Me Your Funny Boot Camp Story

Send me your funny experience about boot camp. No, it may not have been funny then, but looking back it's funny now. If your funny experience is published in the sequel to this book, *Return to Parris Island Daze,* I will include your name (if desired) in the Acknowledgements and mail you an autographed copy of the book.

E-mail your story to my website at ParrisIslandDaze.com.

Share with your buddies how it was in 'the old Corps'.